D1338009

A Pictorial Survey of
RAILWAY
STATIONS

Hensall 1974. LYR Cottage Orné of 1848. Note the hipped gables and the fanciful modillions supporting the eaves.

Denmark Hill 1975. LBSCR Italianate of 1886. Largely destroyed by fire c1980 and since restored.

Telford Central 1986. British Rail of 1986 showing transition from 'slab-roof' modern to post-modern style.

A Pictorial Survey of
RAILWAY
STATIONS

Gordon A. Buck C.Eng. MIEE

BCA
LONDON · NEW YORK · SYDNEY · TORONTO

Somerleyton 1976. GER Tudor of 1847, possibly by John Thomas, to serve the country house of Sir Samuel Morton Peto the railway contractor.

Gloucester 1983. British Rail 1977. The ultimate in BR 'prefab' modern style. Built on the site of Gloucester Central, it also replaced the MR Gloucester Eastgate so that calling north/south trains now have to reverse. The new platform vies in length with that of Cambridge.

© 1992 G. A. Buck & Oxford Publishing Co.

All rights reserved. No part of this book may be reproduced or transmitted in any form or by any means, electronic or mechanical, including photocopying, recording or by any information storage or retrieval system, without written permission from the copyright owner.

This edition published 1992 by BCA by arrangement with Oxford Publishing Co., Sparkford, near Yeovil, Somerset BA22 7JJ.

CN 3154

Printed by: J. H. Haynes & Co. Ltd
Typeset in Times Medium Roman 10/11pt

Contents

Introduction

Railway stations range in size from small private houses to major civic buildings. Their study forms both an introduction to the secular architecture of the last 150 years and an archaeological look at railway history.

This book is a pictorial survey of the architecture of British railway stations as they have stood in the two decades since 1972. It attempts throughout to classify buildings into various styles of architecture to add interest, and as an aid to understanding and appreciation. Accordingly it also attempts to define these styles or at least to give some pointers to their recognition. The more experienced reader will appreciate the limitations of this process which, to some extent, can be arbitrary and occasionally misleading. Ultimately each building has its own design and classification which, like beauty, is in the eye of the beholder.

The approach is broadly chronological by date of construction. Stations are first grouped to illustrate the historical architectural styles favoured by the early Victorians; then come the collected works of the better known railway architects. The emergence of company standard designs and details later in the 19th century follows. The buildings of London's main line termini span both the 19th and 20th centuries and, for the sake of completeness, have a short chapter of their own. They have been admirably and more fully treated elsewhere as indicated in the bibliography. The 20th Century shows first Edwardian consolidation and then the steady trend towards modernism until the Second World War. The last 25 years have seen much station rebuilding in the evolving and contemporary modern manner aiming to attract business to a modern passenger railway, and to reduce the total future cost of ownership by dimensioning appropriate to expected needs and the use of system building techniques and maintenance-free materials.

Continuing development renders futile my original aim to include only buildings surviving at publication and thus save the reader the aggravation of being unable to view any example personally. However, every picture is dated and any building known to have disappeared is noted.

Principal sources of information are listed in the bibliography and I apologize here and now for the inevitable omissions. Acknowledgement is paid to Bryan Morgan and particularly to Gordon Biddle whose works respectively inspired the commencement and comprehensive completion of the photography on which this book is based – and to the administrations of Dr Beeching which provided the motivation.

G.A.B.

Notes:

All photographs are by the author. The date quoted in the caption is when the photograph was taken. Stations illustrated are mentioned in bold type in the text. Some shown in colour and not described in the text have additional information in the caption.

Bibliography

Christian Barman *An Introduction to Railway Architecture* 1950.
John Betjeman & John Gay *London's Historic Railway Stations* 1972 John Murray.
Gordon Biddle *Victorian Stations* 1973 David & Charles.
Gordon Biddle & O. S. Nock *The Railway Heritage of Britain* 1983 Michael Joseph.
Marcus Binney, David Pearce et al. *Railway Architecture* 1979 Orbis Publishing.
M. Bowers & P. Watters *Railway Styles in Building* 1975 Almark
Alan A. Jackson *London's Termini* 1969

Laurence Menear *London's Underground Stations* 1983 Midas Books.
Bryan Morgan *Civil Engineering, Railways.*
Jack Simmons *The Railways of Britain.* 1961. Revised and re-issued 1986 MacMillan.
Nigel Wikeley & John Middleton *Railway Stations – Southern Region.* 1971 Peco Publications.
British Railways Pre-Grouping Atlas and Gazetteer. 1976 Ian Allan.
Railway Magazine Collected issues, particularly post-war.

Note on Abbreviations

To save tedious repetition the principal railway companies, which either built stations or absorbed the smaller companies that did, are referred to by the following initials. At the end of 1922 they were reconstituted into the Big Four companies, LMSR, LNER, SR and GWR which were ultimately nationalized to form the six regions of British Railways.

CR	Caledonian Railway
CLC	Cheshire Lines Committee Railway (Jointly owned by MSLR, GNR and MR)
FR	Furness Railway
GER	Great Eastern Railway
GNR	Great Northern Railway
G&SWR	Glasgow & South Western Railway
GWR	Great Western Railway
HR	Highland Railway
LBSCR	London, Brighton & South Coast Railway
LCDR	London, Chatham & Dover Railway
LMSR	London, Midland & Scottish Railway
LNER	London & North Eastern Railway
LNWR	London & North Western Railway
LSWR	London & South Western Railway
LTSR	London, Tilbury & Southend Railway
LYR	Lancashire & Yorkshire Railway
MR	Midland Railway
MSLR	Manchester, Sheffield & Lincolnshire Railway
NBR	North British Railway
NER	North Eastern Railway
NLR	North London Railway
SR	Southern Railway
SER	South Eastern Railway

Foreword

The railway scene has changed immeasurably in the last 25 years. In 1968 the last steam hauled train had run, giving way to diesel and electric traction, the latter involving intrusive overhead power lines, quite the worst example being the initial phase of the West Coast Main Line electrification. The railway system had been contracting for some years with the closure of many branch lines even before the 1963 Beeching Report which accelerated the process. From that time not even entire main lines, certainly not some of the intermediate stations, were sacrosanct. Modern signalling technology was superseding scores of the once traditional signal boxes. Only the railway station remained as a reminder of the former railway scene. Even these largely Victorian buildings were subject to deterioration or had outgrown their original purpose, hence there were many cases of partial or entire demolition and rebuilding in a modern style.

This dramatic change in the railway environment provided Gordon Buck with the incentive to record photographically the stations that survived, whether original or rebuilt. With the 1976 BR timetable as his reference point he set out to record every station on the system, and having succeeded in that objective, he has turned his attention to stations in Ireland and on the Continent, as well as to noteworthy railway structures.

This book depicts the changing scene over 150 years of railway stations in England, Scotland and Wales. The lavish selection of photographs is augmented by accounts of some of the more noteworthy architects and individual railway styles right to the present day.

In the 1960s BR went through a bad patch environmentally — who can forgive them the destruction of the so called Doric Arch at Euston or even the construction of such atrocities as Birmingham New Street? Elsewhere on the network considerable staff reductions led to increasing neglect. Adverse criticism resulted in the appointment of Bernard Kaukas ARIBA as BR Director of Environment in 1977 by the then Chairman, Sir Peter Parker. This was followed in 1985 by the creation of the Railway Heritage Trust with the mandate to liaise between BR and outside parties with an awareness of their heritage, ie local authorities, and the ability to award grants towards the restoration of BR stations in daily use. These two factors have led to a dramatic increase in the refurbishment of railway stations. A notable example is the rebuilt Liverpool Street station opened by Her Majesty The Queen in 1991.

Thus the station scene is an ongoing one. It is not generally realised that BR is the custodian of over one thousand listed structures and this number regularly increases. Gordon Buck's efforts, very time consuming and costly, present a worthy record of notable railway stations over the last fifteen years. When he set out on his monumental task there were 2,400 stations named in the timetable. This book is commended to anyone with an interest in railways and their architecture.

R. C. Riley

Battle 1974

Left and below **Battle 1980**

I Nineteenth Century Styles of Architecture

". . . in the early years of the nineteenth century the fancy-dress ball of architecture is in full swing: Classical, Gothic, Italianate, Old English. By 1840 pattern books for builders and clients include many more styles: Tudor, French Renaissance and others." Nikolaus Pevsner.

Victorian historicism provides a resumé of all pre-existing forms of architecture in this country; not necessarily correct in every detail, and often confusingly mixed, because the Victorians were eclectics and their wish to incorporate the best bits was seldom inhibited by disciplines earlier regarded as inviolable. Increasingly, as

the century passed, architects were evolving contemporary forms of their own.

Over the ages British architecture, like the British people, has been so much influenced by a succession of invaders that it is almost impossible to define a truly native form. Nevertheless Tudor and its derivatives seem decidedly more English than Classical and Italianate. Tudor was based on earlier vernacular buildings, in timber or stone as dictated by the availability of materials. Classical was a later import of European Renaissance.

1 Gothic

In church building English Gothic evolved from earlier Saxon and Norman practice. The three phases of its development, Early English, Decorated and Perpendicular need not be elaborated here. Victorian Gothic revival, particularly for secular buildings, tended to combine features of the first two forms to provide simpler and more robust structures.

Battle station is the epitome of early Gothic styling and incorporates features to be found in small churches built as early as the 13th Century or as late as the 19th. It was erected in 1852 for the SER and is one of a series of stations designed by William Tress for that company on the lines from Hastings to Ashford and to Tunbridge Wells. The style may well have been adopted here as a sympathetic gesture to the nearby Battle Abbey. The exterior has an appropriate doorway and windows with simple plate tracery. Inside, the booking hall has an open collar-braced roof and the doorway to the platform is sheltered beneath a small arcade. The platform elevation was spoilt about the turn of the century by the addition of a canopy.

Middlesbrough was built in 1877 when the Victorian Gothic revival was at its height. It is accordingly more elaborate than Battle and has rose windows and a renaissance parapet at the roof line. But it still eschews the extremes of High Victorian Gothic. In the booking hall is an example of a true hammerbeam roof; purists might regard the tie-rods as cheating a bit. Originally the platforms were partly covered by an unusually high iron and glass overall roof but this has been removed following damage by enemy action. The architect was William Peachey of the NER.

Left and below **Middlesbrough 1975**

2 Tudor

Original Tudor and Elizabethan buildings can sometimes be distinguished by differences of detail if the date of construction is in doubt. Victorian Tudor usually embodies features from both and, indeed, Elizabethan often predominates, but it is now usual and convenient to refer to it as Tudor. In many ways it can be regarded as the domestic partner of ecclesiastical Gothic and, although sometimes used for large buildings, Tudor is typically the basis of very many splendid little stations built by early railways. It is characterized by doorways with rather flat pointed arches, steeply pitched roofs, tall and decorative chimneys and upper windows set in gables extended up from the walls. The gables themselves are haunched to provide a complete stop to the roofs and eaves. Label dripstones are often added over windows and, in more pretentious buildings, larger 'perpendicular' windows and oriels may also be used. Occasionally overall façades are symmetrical in the renaissance manner but balanced asymmetry in the 'English' style is more usual.

Wateringbury was built by the SER, probably in 1855, on its line from Paddock Wood to Strood. It is an outstanding example of a small Tudor country station. Note the angled chimneys, the haunched gables, the pointed arch to the doorway and the upper window set in a gable. **Aylesford,** on the same line, is very similar but built in Kentish ragstone. It would have the greater merit of the two had it not lost its chimneys. Very recently it has been restored. Another look is recommended.

Barnes is another attractive station, built by the LSWR in 1846 to the design of Sir William Tite. The brick box extension added later on the left is nothing to do with Sir William.

Cheddleton and **Rushton** were both stations of the North Staffordshire Railway built in 1849. The former is now in the hands of a railway preservation society.

Wateringbury 1978

Barnes 1975

Cuxton was built by the SER in 1856 on the same line as Wateringbury. It shows how the style can be adapted to a single storey building. The lozenge-paned windows are not a SER exclusive: the MR also used them, for example at Beeston.

All the foregoing show the characteristic features of small Tudor railway stations. **Atherstone** is slightly larger and well justifies its recent refurbishment. It incorporates some octagonal chimneys and an oriel window on the left. It was designed by J. W. Livock and built by the Trent Valley Railway (later part of the LNWR) in 1847. The station is unstaffed and the building has been out of use for railway purposes for some years. Its rehabilitation and use as offices is an excellent piece of conservation.

Lincoln Central is bigger still. It was built by J. Taylor in 1848 for the GNR. It is unusually grand for that company who tended to favour small Italianate buildings. Perhaps it was to vie with the classical Saint Marks station of the MR (now closed and demolished) to provide a worthy railhead for the city. In addition to continuous drip-stones it features pointed doorways, an oriel window and, in the tower, a slightly incongruous blind rose window.

Ripon was built by the NER in 1848. It is a Victorian cocktail. A fine Gothic entrance combines with windows that mix Gothic with Tudor. Ball finials and chimney pots add to the confusion. But over the windows you can see just what 'label' drip stones should look like.

11

Cuxton
1975

Atherstone
1989

Lincoln
Central
1977

3 Jacobean

The Elizabethan period was followed by the Jacobean. Increasing Dutch influence at that time manifested itself most obviously in the introduction of ogee shaped gables. At the same time the wish for a fireplace in nearly every room led to a proliferation of chimney flues much more closely grouped than in the Elizabethan practice. Victorian stations in the Jacobean manner are accordingly characterized by ogee gables, chunkily grouped chimneys and a rather freer treatment of windows. Usually the roofs are slightly less steeply pitched.

Wansford station was another designed by J. W. Livock for the LNWR and was erected in 1845. It has a fine display of gables but the chimneys are, unfortunately, no longer in character. The upper parts of chimneys are always at risk, particularly when built of stone, as a result of the effects of weather aggravated by the corrosive products of combustion. Consequent repairs have often subordinated character to economy.

Maldon East has much the air of a renaissance manor house. It was built in 1846 and now survives to accommodate a builders merchant. An arcade on the ground floor provided a sheltered entrance and the floor above carries a splendid range of characteristic chimneys and gables. It is amazing that such a building could be justified at the end of a small branch line. Presumably the euphoria of the railway mania of the 1840s which led to the construction of many scarcely necessary lines would allow managements the indulgence of a scarcely necessary building or two.

Louth was designed by Weightman and Hadfield for the East Lincolnshire Railway and built in 1848. The company was acquired by the GNR who thus gained a station that completely outclassed their normally unambitious Italianate ones. Since closure the building has deteriorated and even been threatened with demolition but there are some efforts to retain and restore it.

Maldon East 1977

Louth 1973

Brocklesby, 1848, and **Worksop**, 1849, are both on the former MSLR system. The elaboration at Brocklesby, sited in the back of beyond, becomes less surprising when the presence of Brocklesby Hall, just over the horizon to the south, is taken into account. It was quite usual to provide the local land-owner with a station that he could be proud of. In this case he was also the chairman of the railway.

Ellesmere Port is a later example built in 1863 by the Birkenhead Joint Railway. The chimneys here have been rebuilt in a properly detailed way although the corbelling of the tops seems slightly exaggerated. It gives a feeling of top-heaviness particularly in the case of the single flue. In fact, however, owing to the inscrutable law of gravity and the rules of masonry, the added mass actually increases stability.

Brocklesby 1977

Worksop 1972

Ellesmere Port 1976

4 Cottage Orné

An important factor in Victorian architecture was the pursuit of the picturesque and this is at its most obvious in the style known as Cottage Orné. Although undoubtedly inspired by English vernacular architecture Cottage Orné is really a Victorian invention in its own right. The principal features are the fantastically pierced and ornamented barge boards which usually feature finials and often pendants at the peaks of gables. The buildings may be stone or brick but more usually are half or fully timbered, but the exposed timbering is largely and sometimes entirely cosmetic.

The Bedford Railway constructed what became a LNWR branch line from Bletchley to Bedford in 1846.

Much of it traversed the Duke of Bedford's Woburn estate and it may be the stations were done in Cottage Orné style for his pleasure. None of the estate's present buildings seem to be in this style however. **Fenny Stratford** is the best of the bunch and is also the best surviving station in this style in the land. Note how the first floor is jettied out from the ground floor in the timber framed manner but note also that the joists appear to be Victorian deal rather than medieval oak. Slightly smaller variants are to be found at **Ridgmont**, Woburn Sands and **Millbrook**. Some of the other stations on the line were in brick and incorporated a cruck-shaped motif in the end wall. Of these only Lidlington survives.

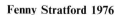

Fenny Stratford 1976

Betchworth of 1849 by the SER has appropriate barge boards but less exposed timber. The tile hanging may have been added later as was done at many LBSCR stations in Sussex of the Sheffield Park type. Betchworth also has attractive semi-dormer windows breaking the roof line.

The North Western Railway in Lancashire also used timbered styling in the Cottage Orné manner at several stations including **Clapham** and Giggleswick built in 1849. The railway was known as The Little North Western to distinguish it from the LNWR. It became, in fact, part of the Midland Railway.

Betchworth 1974

5 Classical

This book includes among classically styled buildings those in the Classical Revival manner, complete with orders of columns, pediments, etc., together with the progressively more sober derivatives, Renaissance and neo-Georgian. Baroque can be distinguished from Classical architecture as being more elaborately decorative and, although Victorian buildings often include Baroque features, completely Baroque buildings became more in vogue in the 20th Century Edwardian era, at least for railway stations. French Renaissance is identified separately.

Classical façades are normally symmetrical and great attention is paid to the proportions of the openings and their disposition and to the proportions of the whole composition. Pythagoras, of right angle triangle fame, among others, noticed that physical proportions having the same numerical ratios as those connecting the notes of the musical scale produced aesthetically pleasing results. Three of the most obvious are 1:1, 1:$\sqrt{2}$ or approximately 5:7, like the 'A' series of paper sizes, and 1:2. Interestingly the golden number or golden section which also produces very satisfactory results is not a harmonic ratio. Its value is $\frac{\sqrt{5}+1}{2}$ or approximately 5:8.

The principal storey (the Italian piano nobile) is the first floor and its windows will receive the grandest treatment, often being adorned with pediments to act as drip stones. In English practice the ground floor is sometimes half buried to become a full or semi-basement bringing the principal storey closer to ground level. It can then incorporate the main entrance reached by a short staircase.

Designed by J. P. Pritchett, **Huddersfield** was built in 1847 jointly for the LYR and the Huddersfield & Manchester Railway & Canal Company (later part of the LNWR). It is our outstanding example of a Palladian Classical station and a credit to the city which takes pride in its civic buildings and saw to it that the station survived. The central building has a pedimented Corinthian portico and the window bays are marked by Corinthian pilasters. The ends of the roof are also treated as pediments. On either hand are symmetrical small pavilions linked to the centre by colonnades. The parapet above the cornice of each pavilion is given freer treatment and carries the seal of one of the participating companies.

Thomas Moore designed **Monkwearmouth**, built in 1848. It is on the North bank of the River Wear and was once the terminus of the Brandling Junction Railway. An Ionic portico is combined with freely treated Doric wings. Although trains pass through, its role is now a museum of railway artefacts.

Above, right and below
Huddersfield 1988

Monkwearmouth 1988

Birmingham Curzon Street was built in 1838 to form the other end of the London & Birmingham Railway. Philip Hardwick gave it a Greek Revival Ionic frontage as a balance to the Doric entrance to Euston. It has been restored and is now in non-railway use as offices.

Southampton Terminus was built by Sir William Tite in 1840 to form the country end of the London & Southampton Railway from Nine Elms in London. This is the epitome of English Renaissance styling. The orders of columns have disappeared but note how the roofline is treated as a cornice with dentils beneath it, the first floor enhanced with pediments to the windows and the entrance marked by a Roman arcade surmounted by a balustrade. The ground floor is rusticated, the stonework joints being exaggerated by cutting back, to give a feeling of greater solidity. The reduction in the height of the openings on each successive storey also contributes stability and serenity.

Newark Castle is now the oldest surviving classical station by the MR. Built in 1846, it shows how a satisfactory composition can be achieved even in a single storey. Flat pediments to the windows and restrained pilasters at the entrance all contribute.

The MSLR was capable of both restraint and ostentation. **Market Rasen**, 1848, and Gainsborough Central, 1849, both had rather unimposing single storey buildings. Market Rasen has a restrained classical entrance its doorway framed in pilasters supporting a cornice. Within it once had an overall roof, now gone. **Gainsborough Central** had a splendid Roman style portico although latterly it was out of use. Nothing now remains there but unstaffed platforms.

The MR's **Ashby-de-la-Zouch** station of 1849 is more elaborate than Newark. Here the single storey consists of a Greek Doric entrance block flanked by slightly smaller pavilions. It is now conserved as commercial offices.

Birmingham Curzon Street 1988

Southampton Terminus 1975

Newark Castle 1977

Market Rasen 1977

Gainsborough Central 1976

Ashby-de-la-Zouch 1988

20

Gravesend was built in 1849 by the SER and has been cleaned and refurbished of late. It is a pleasing composition of twin pavilions linked by a Doric colonnade. Purists might find the frieze rather too deep and the imposed balustrade out of place. Canterbury West is less imposing but its Doric entrance is done more correctly.

Wakefield Kirkgate, 1857, was a joint station for the GNR and the LYR. It shows the effect on an originally splendidly restrained symmetry of pandering to operational needs.

George Smith designed the original terminus at the outer end of the London & Greenwich Railway in 1838.

When the railway was extended it had to be moved. The present **Greenwich** building, of 1875, one of the SER's finest in Renaissance form, is said to be a faithful copy of Smith's. But not the box on the right. The first floor windows, being the same height as the ground floor ones, seem to give the building a slightly top heavy feeling.

Bath Green Park was built by the MR in 1870 on its route from the Midlands to Bournemouth. Its late Renaissance style complements and compliments the city it faces and it put one over the GWR's Bath Spa. It is well conserved as a supermarket car park by a well known grocer's who pay attention to architecture.

Gravesend 1983

Wakefield Kirkgate 1977

Greenwich 1975

Bath Green Park 1988

Norwich Thorpe 1976

Norwich Thorpe 1979

6 French Renaissance

The French Renaissance style conforms to classical symmetry but with added, almost Baroque, decoration. To see it in full flower requires a visit to France. In English railway practice it is mainly and sometimes solely characterised by mansard pavilion roofs, either straight sided or curved to form a four-sided 'dome'. Main pediments are absent and sometimes substituted by a decorative clock gable.

Although some hotels are larger **Norwich** is our best French Renaissance station. It was built in 1886 by the GER to the design of its Engineer, John Wilson and his architectural assistant W. N. Ashbee. Moulded bricks are incorporated in the pillars of the porte-cochère to imitate rustication. Inside, a carefully restored entrance leads to a travel centre and a rather cluttered but basically spacious concourse.

Portsmouth and Southsea served the LBSCR and LSWR jointly and they rebuilt it in 1866. It is a Victorian sandwich with French above and Italianate below. The cantilevered porte-cochère is resplendent with iron founders' art.

Welshpool was designed by Benjamin Piercy and built in 1860 by the Oswestry & Newtown Railway as its headquarters. The railway was absorbed by the GWR and the station is too large for today's needs.

Teignmouth, built about 1880, is a GWR standard design here executed in snecked rubble. Note the cast iron cresting to the pavilion roofs, an integral feature of the design which does not survive everywhere. **Torquay** was

Right and below
Portsmouth and Southsea 1978

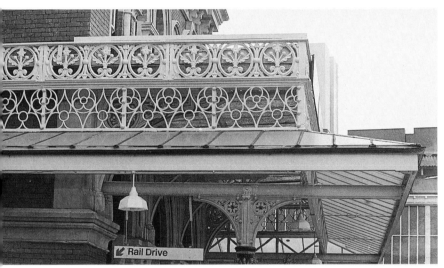

Welshpool 1976

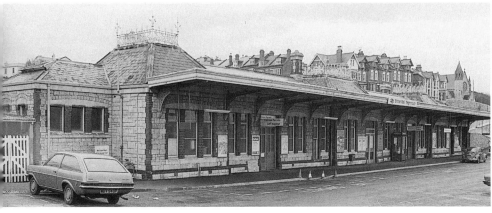

Teignmouth 1977

23

built at the same time and is a variant enlarged to incorporate an integral footbridge connecting similar buildings on both sides of the line.

Slough was designed by J. Danks of the GWR and built in 1886. Like Torquay it has similar buildings on both sides of the station but otherwise is like a small simplified copy of Nice. Note the round dormers (oeil de boeuf) in the pavilion roofs. It is much the best of the GWR's French style stations.

Left and below
Torquay 1977

Below
Slough 1979

Slough 1979

7 Italianate

Between them, the Italianate and Tudor styles accounted for the great majority of early small stations. Italianate is characterised by round headed window openings, often grouped in twos and threes, and shallow pitched roofs, at much the same angle as a classical pediment. The roofs were usually, but not always, hipped. Although façades are only occasionally symmetrical, Italianate can conveniently be regarded as the domestic partner of corporate classical buildings just as Tudor partners Gothic.

Gobowen is the archetypical Italianate station, complete with campanile turret. It was built by the Shrewsbury & Chester Railway (later, GWR) in 1846 to the design of T. K. Penson who is perhaps better remembered for Shrewsbury.

Different railways varied the style somewhat as the fancy took them. SER practice can be seen at **Walmer**, 1881, and **Chislehurst**, 1901. Chislehurst's cresting, already shaky in 1975, has now been removed. Tonbridge once had a rather similar building on its overbridge but it was replaced, unfortunately, by the present building when simplification was fashionable.

The GNR used Italianate styling almost exclusively. Surviving stations show no signs of standardization in this style. **Welwyn North**, 1853, is reasonably typical. **Wood Green**, 1859, now known as Alexandra Palace, has a chimney anticipating Domestic Revival. Its polychrome brickwork is exceptional for the GNR.

The GER's **Lowestoft**, 1847, shows the depths to which Italianate could sink but the campanile turret is good. Inside, the concourse has a wooden overall roof.

Gobowen 1976

Walmer 1975

Chislehurst 1975

Welwyn North 1977

Wood Green 1976

8 Domestic Revival

Domestic Revival acknowledges its basis in Tudor and other English Vernacular architecture. But it is really a late Victorian invention in its own right. It is distinguished by half timbered gables and decorative, usually rather massive chimneys in moulded brick. It may also incorporate 'school board' windows, a type in which the upper third is given a chequer pattern of panes by additional glazing bars. Roofs are mostly of intermediate pitch, neither as steep as Tudor nor as shallow as Georgian or Italianate. Each railway company that practised the style had its own version for by the time it was in vogue, 1890 to 1905 roughly, corporate identities were being expressed in buildings.

Sandling, 1888, was once the junction for the branch to Hythe on the SER. A fully timbered example with brick nogging and at least one characteristic chimney, it has a gabled hip roof reminiscent of a Wealden hall house.

The GER used a rather plain version without impos-

ing chimneys but having the characteristic timbered gable. The wing walls backing the platform often end in ogee shapes. Several can be found on the Essex coastal lines. **Prittlewell**, 1889, is typical.

The MR used a very idiosyncratic version and indulged its fancy for terracotta in the facings. A monogrammatic MR substitutes timbering in the gable. **Kettering** of 1890 is illustrated. Rotherham Masborough was very similar but has now been closed.

Bromborough is an archetypical example. The Birkenhead Joint Railway (GWR/LNWR) used this as a standard design at many stations about 1895.

The Wirral Railway built **West Kirby** in 1896 and gave it an out-of-character clock tower.

Streatham Common of 1890 shows the approach of the LBSCR. The gables are adorned with circular windows instead of timbering. Norbury, Selhurst and Thornton Heath are similar.

**Prittlewell
1977**

*Above
and left*
**Kettering
1978**

Bromborough 1976

**West
Kirby
1976**

**Streatham
Common 1980**

II Works of Early Railway Architects

The North Eastern Railway, more than most, consistently used the services of architects. Most of the stations of two of its earliest constituents, the Newcastle & Carlisle Railway and the Newcastle & Berwick Railway were designed by Benjamin Green. In the same period G. T. Andrews was designing stations for the rest of its system. At mid-century Thomas Prosser took over, giving way in turn to William Bell in 1847. He carried on the good work almost until the NER became part of the LNER in the reorganisation at the end of 1922.

1 Benjamin Green

John G. Green and his son Benjamin were in partnership as architects in Newcastle. Benjamin Green's first railway work was on the Newcastle & Carlisle Railway in 1835. **Wylam, Gilsland** and **Brampton** were all in a railway Tudor style with a central jettied dormer and correct drip stones on the ground floor windows. Each had additional buildings appended. The old name Brampton Junction recalls that it was once the junction for a branch line to Brampton itself but the buildings no longer exist here. Buildings at Low Row and Riding Mill are similar but others are varied in style. A ticket window, once accessible from the platform, survives at Gilsland.

Twelve years later, in 1847, Green built for the Newcastle & Berwick Railway a series of more elaborate Tudor stations complete with semi-dormers, bay windows and even an occasional oriel. They all had ball finials to their gables and the style might, therefore, be termed Tudor-with-knobs-on. The platform shelters were mostly formed by extending a main roof in a catslide and supporting the outer edge with decorative wooden supports.

Longhirst, **Stannington**, Acklington and **Warkworth** survive in private hands. The elevated Warkworth, reached by a stone staircase, is particularly fine. Morpeth, **Acklington** (unstaffed platforms only), and **Chathill** are still operational. The entrance arcade at **Morpeth** has been enclosed and an alternative entrance created in the linking block. **Belford** is the only one to preserve its entrance in pristine state. It is vacant but used by the railway as a depot. **Beal**, once the station for Holy Island, has been demolished. The surviving Longhirst is fairly similar to it. Other surviving buildings are in a simpler style and/or smaller.

Wylam 1975

Gilsland 1975

Brampton 1975

Stannington 1976

Warkworth 1975

Acklington 1975

31

Chathill 1976

Morpeth 1973

Left and below
Belford 1976

Beal 1976

2 George Townsend Andrews

G. T. Andrews of York is chiefly remembered for his railway work. He was a friend of George Hudson the 'Railway King' and was employed extensively by the principal precursor of the NER, the York & North Midland Railway.

At **Scarborough** Andrews used a classical composition of three pavilions. It was built in 1844. The central Baroque clock tower is nothing to do with his design,

having been added in 1884. Inside the overall roof is constructed of standard components but ad hoc extensions have made the station untidy.

Malton, 1845, has large twin pavilions whose link shelters beneath an extension of the overall roof. Such a roof sheltering a single through platform is now rare and at Malton it uniquely serves trains in either direction.

Scarborough 1981

Malton 1974

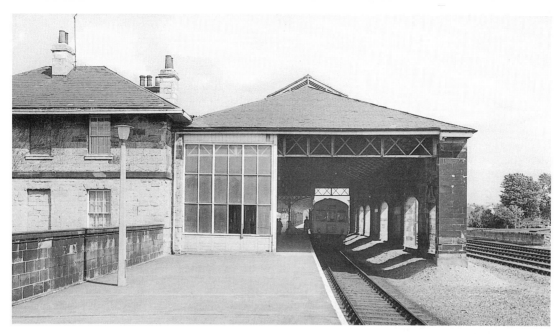

Left and below **Malton 1974**

Beverley, of 1846, has a quietly classical entrance block with the roofline treated as a cornice supported on modillions. The delicate wrought iron and glass awning is a later addition. Inside is the only complete example in railway use of an overall roof once widely used on the NER. It has a hipped slated form and at the Southern end is a nice NER pattern covered footbridge.

Driffield of the same year has an arcade to the Northbound platform. Its overall roof has been dismantled.

Beverley 1974

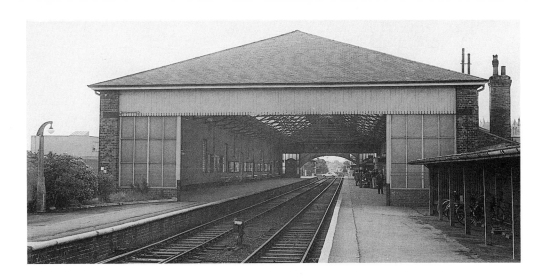

Above, left and below
Beverley 1974

Driffield 1978

Filey's roof was partly gone in 1974 and reveals something of the construction. It was also built in 1846 and has a standard open NER footbridge.

Market Weighton built in 1847 and probably now demolished, had a Doric entrance.

Pocklington, 1847, also had classical tendencies, this time with a Roman arcaded entrance or loggia. The overall roofed interior is complete and has been converted into a gymnasium; conservation at its best.

Andrews' smaller stations have a more or less Italianate air. **Hutton Cranswick**, particularly, looks to have strayed from the GNR. Built in 1846, it shows the mild classical doorway provided at stations that did not qualify for the more imposing porch. Examples survive at Haxby and Barton Hill. Slightly larger stations of 1847, such as **Nafferton, Lockington** and **Bempton** had a three bay main block at right angles to the railway and a classical porch on Doric pillars. Another survivor was noted at Stamford Bridge in 1985. This and Bempton are mirror versions and the latter shows how altered windows spoil the appearance however much they may suit the occupier. A year earlier, at **Castle Howard**, to serve the big house, Andrews had elaborated the same basic design into a Baroque Italianate complete with a broken verge to the roof facing the platform.

On the Whitby & Pickering Railway a more Tudor style was used with fancy, Cottage Orné bargeboards and finials. All were built in 1847. **Grosmont** is now in the hands of the North Yorkshire Moors Railway.

Filey 1974

Pocklington 1974

Hutton Cranswick 1978

Nafferton 1974

Lockington 1978

Bempton 1978

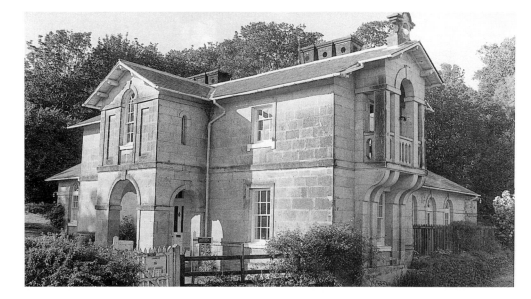

Castle Howard 1985

Grosmont 1978

Sleights was identical but has had a careful extension on the right of the platform elevation. Ruswarp is a variant but bears the appropriate bargeboards and openings. Whitby itself has classical arcaded elevations.

Terminal stations traditionally had their main buildings adjacent to the departure platform and not across the head behind the buffer stops as seems more usual today. This is where Andrews' original renaissance building of 1848 is to be found at Hull Paragon. Tucked away on the south side, it is apt to be forgotten. Andrews built the Royal Station Hotel across the head of the station in

1851. It is a nicely proportioned renaissance building with a modillioned cornice and rusticated quoins. In 1936 it was totally surrounded, on either side and above, by extensions.

The older buildings at Durham, of 1857, were completed by Prosser but are probably to Andrews' design. The 'up' side building has a three-bay Tudor porch and, like the more extensive 'down' side, other Tudor details. Passengers now use a separate pre-fab style entry and booking office on the 'up' side.

Sleights 1978

**Ruswarp
1974**

**Whitby
1974**

Hull Paragon 1984

**Hull.
Royal
Station
Hotel
1972**

*Left and
below*
**Durham
1981**

3 John Dobson

John Dobson had been principally involved as architect and planner in setting out central **Newcastle** and he was commissioned by the NER to design its station there. It was built in 1850 and is symmetrical about the central portico. The massive combination of arcading with a cornice, frieze and pilasters in Doric style gives a Baroque effect. The portico functions as a porte-cochère and closely harmonizes with the rest of the building. It was completed by Prosser later, when the railway had moved its headquarters from Newcastle to York, and commanded him to economize. Dobson had planned a much more imposing and ornate one in Corinthian style.

It is perhaps well to note, in passing, that the term porte-cochère properly describes a door or gateway giving vehicle access to an inner courtyard as in coaching inn practice. The term is commonly extended, as here, to mean a carriage porch under which travellers can transfer from vehicle to building in shelter.

Dobson's three-bay train shed, later added to, was the very first to have roofs supported by rolled iron ribs tied with light rods. The curving vista along the principal platforms is of unequalled splendour.

The **Royal Station Hotel**, 1854, adjoins the station proper to the east. The main section has four floors below the cornice, then a two-storey attic surmounted by a garret with pedimented dormers above a second cornice. The entrance block has some French touches. To its left the composition lacks the expected symmetry and is, presumably, part of the extension of 1892.

Newcastle 1978

Newcastle 1973

Newcastle 1978

Newcastle. Royal Station
Hotel 1983

Newcastle. Royal Station
Hotel 1973

4 Thomas Prosser

Thomas Prosser was the first staff architect of the NER and served from 1857 to 1874. After completing Newcastle he continued the policy, introduced by Andrews, of a degree of standardisation but using his own designs.

At **Saltburn**, 1861, he used polychrome brick and as a centre-piece provided an entrance portico in Roman style. Note the glazing bars of the windows in the form

of a Venetian arch. The train shed within covered two tracks but only one platform. The colonnaded recess at the back of the platform and the simple tied rafter roof, using trussed rafters are standard features. Beyond the train shed rails and platform once extended to the rear of the Zetland Hotel, served by occasional through carriages. Only an unstaffed excursion platform survives.

Saltburn 1978 (Four views)

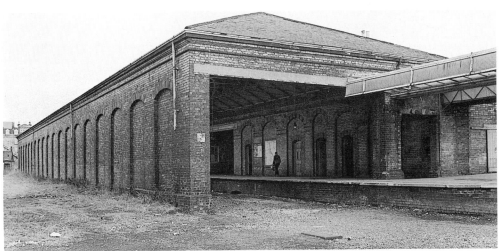

Redcar, 1863, is predominately Italianate and is symmetrical. The now-enclosed porte-cochère is not Prosser's fault. The interior is a single-track shed like Saltburn's but, unlike Malton, 'up' trains use a separate open platform.

Bishop Auckland, 1863, had a lighter single track train shed and was once a junction on the Stockton & Darlington Railway. Trains from Darlington now terminate at a platform with a small post-modern building. All else is gone.

Above, left and below
Redcar Central 1978

Bishop Auckland 1975

Danby, Lealholm, Glaisdale and Egton, all of 1865, show standardization on the Whitby line. Built in coursed rubble, they have crowstepped gables occasionally found in Northern England. In Scotland they would be commonplace and usually steeper.

York was designed by Prosser but completed in 1877 by Peachey. Segmental arches for the arcaded porte-cochère seem at odds with the balustrade above. As built, without the street canopy and partial glazing, it probably looked better and would have echoed the lower frontage of King's Cross at the time. Crescent glazed end screens complete a splendid train shed built, like Newcastle, on a curve. The iron ribs of the roof have decorative perforations in their webs and are supported on chunky Corinthian columns surmounted by spandrel brackets bearing the arms of York.

Danby 1978

Lealholm 1978

Glaisdale 1978

Egton 1978

Left and below **York 1972**

Right and below
York 1972

5 William Peachey

Peachey served as NER architect from 1876 to 1877. He followed Prossor's immediate successor, Benjamin Burleigh, none of whose work is included here.

While completing York station Peachey designed and built the adjoining **Royal Station Hotel**, also completed in 1877. His principal work is Middlesbrough, described earlier.

York. Royal Station Hotel 1972

6 William Bell

William Bell succeeded Peachey and served the NER practically until its submersion in the LNER in 1923. In his day clock towers were becoming fashionable but in many of his surviving stations the interiors are, perhaps, of more interest.

Darlington Bank Top, 1887, is an island platform station serving through trains on its outer faces and having bay platforms between for terminating ones. The whole is enclosed in an overall roof of three bays. The platform and offices are reached by subway from a porte-cochère entrance dominated by a clock tower with baroque features.

The outside of **Stockton**, 1893, was a Romanesque porte-cochère. It had side platforms. Until 1979 there was an overall roof like Darlington's but lacking its symmetry.

In 1904 at **Hull Paragon** Bell provided an extensive new train shed following, by now, well-established NER practice. The wooden art-nouveau buildings on the concourse are also of interest but the outstanding feature is the lantern lit entrance and booking office. The exterior is now disguised as an office block.

Above, left and below
Darlington Bank Top 1973

**Stockton
1975**

Left and below
**Hull Paragon
1972**

Hull Paragon 1984

Hull Paragon 1972

Manors, 1909, had terracotta facings the MR might have liked in late Domestic Revival with a superimposed clock turret. The building is no more and the station is largely superseded by the nearby Tyne & Wear Metro station of the same name.

Whitley Bay, 1910, and Bridlington, 1912, have, respectively a clock tower and clock gable in appropri-ately Edwardian Baroque. **Bridlington** has a pleasant concourse under a light-weight NER roof. Even on through stations the NER rather liked concourses. At **Monkseaton**, 1915, platform and concourse share a NER barrel roof. Whitley Bay and Monkseaton now house the Metro.

Manors
1978

Whitley Bay 1975

Left and above
Bridlington 1974

Monkseaton 1975

7 Francis Thompson

Francis Thompson seems to have been an artistically inclined tailor who opportunistically became a railway architect. His work extensively influenced station building across the breadth of the country from East Anglia to North Wales. All his surviving stations have an Italianate flavour and a few are classical. Many have, or originally had, the feature of an awning supported between pavilions flanking the main block.

The **Midland Hotel** at **Derby**, 1841, is the oldest purpose-built railway hotel in the world. The porch is a very recent addition but Thompson would, no doubt, have approved. Along with it, Thompson built the original Derby station, now twice replaced. Like Cambridge, four years later, it was single-sided.

In 1845 Thompson produced a whole series of stations for the Eastern Counties Railway, the main constituent of the GER. **Bishops Stortford** showed the basic characteristics of a main block with twin, small, pavilions. One had disappeared by 1977 to make way for a glass box booking hall. This side of the building would normally face the platform. Perhaps this was the case before the line was extended to Cambridge. **Audley End** is more obviously Italianate and here the pavilions are replaced by wing walls to support the awning over the platform. At the front is a fine little porte-cochère provided for the pleasure of the local landowner, Lord Braybrooke, who had the big house nearby. He also required the digging of Audley End Tunnel so that the railway would not spoil his view. **Great Chesterford** was a stretched, five-bay, version of Audley End, more severely classical and not quite so appealing. **Shelford** and **Lakenheath** exemplify a more or less standard design, widely used in East Anglia, with small pavilions carrying the platform shelter. Other survivors are less complete. The blank panel on the first floor may have been intended to carry the station name.

Derby. Midland Hotel 1988

Bishops Stortford 1977

Right and below
Audley End 1973

Great Chesterford 1973

Shelford 1977

Lakenheath 1977

Cambridge is the only station built and still worked as a single-sided one, having a long platform ($\frac{1}{4}$ mile) serving trains in both directions, end to end, if necessary simultaneously. The central part of the frontage was originally a classical, open arcaded, porte-cochère. It was enclosed for more internal accommodation forty or so years ago and has since been refurbished. Its spandrels carry roundels displaying the various armorial bearings of the constituent colleges of the University. Like Ely, Cambridge has been attributed to Sancton Wood. It may be he was a senior architect of the GER at the time and would be credited with the work of consultants or junior staff. **Ely**, 1847, has a twin pavilion classical form not unlike a simplified North Woolwich. The flanking buildings are probably later accretions.

1848 saw the completion of a series of stations for the Chester & Holyhead Railway, soon to be part of the LNWR. **Chester** itself, combining classical symmetry with Italianate detailing, is Thompson's largest and best surviving station. It was jointly for the Shrewsbury & Chester railway and was single-sided. The flagstaff marks the centre of its elongated frontage. The central part has a two-storey block linking pavilions each crowned by two Italianate turrets and having arcades at ground level, one open and one enclosed. Above each arcade is a Venetian window with a balustraded balcony. Doubtless, Thompson did not foresee the out-of-centre clock.

Left and below
Cambridge 1988

Ely 1978

Chester 1983

Chester 1973

After Chester, **Flint** is the best surviving Chester & Holyhead station still in operation. The symmetry of **Holywell Junction** is spoilt by a later small building on the right. In very formal Italianate, it represents the apogee of Thompson's 'flanking pavilion' style. It has lost its platform awning and is used only as a house. **Mostyn** is effectively a classical version of Flint but is now derelict.

Rhyl seems less satisfactory; the polychrome brickwork and segmentally arched openings are at odds with the classical frieze and cornice. Thompson's **Bangor** is a bit lost at the end of lots of later buildings. It retains its Italianate belfry and its CH monogrammed roundels. **Bodorgan** has a standard building much used in North Wales. The station name is empanelled not on the house but on the

Left and below
Flint 1976

Holywell Junction 1973

Right and below
Mostyn 1976

Rhyl 1976

Left and above
Bangor 1981

**Bodorgan
1976**

Llong 1976

form wall. **Llong** and Valley are other examples.

More work was done for the GER in the third quarter of the century. **Wrabness**, 1854, on the Harwich line, has characteristic little pavilions on the platform elevation and the frontage receives pavilion treatment in bas-relief. **Mistley** and **Dovercourt** are on the same line and are contemporary. It is reasonable to suppose they too are by Thompson although they are not quite his usual style and they have not been ascribed to him; might they be by Sancton Wood?

Melton, Darsham and **Oulton Broad South**, 1859, are on the East Suffolk line of the GER. Melton, recently re-opened, unstaffed, after years of closure has some of the features of Flint and Mostyn. Darsham and Oulton Broad have awnings on two sides supported on wing walls. Marlesford, on the former Framlingham branch and still to be seen beside the A12, is similar and, like Oulton Broad, has belfried chimneys.

The following decade saw Thompson's final development of a standard station widely used with very minor variations on the GER lines in Essex. **Weeley**, 1866, owing something to both Bodorgan and Wrabness, is typical. **Thorpe-le-Soken** and **Kirby Cross** show some variations. Great Bentley, Alresford and Hythe are other members of the family.

Right and below
Wrabness 1976

Mistley 1976

**Dovercourt
1976**

Melton 1976

**Darsham
1974**

Oulton Broad South 1976

Left and below
Weeley 1977

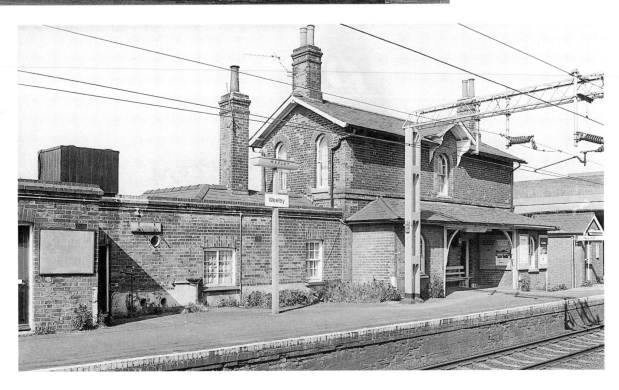

Above and right
Thorpe-le-Soken 1977

Kirby Cross 1977

8 Frederic Barnes

Frederic Barnes of Ipswich designed a series of individual stations built in 1846 for the Ipswich & Bury Railway (GER). Four survive with a train service but some buildings are in non-railway use. Each incorporates a mixture of styles and achieves distinction for the railway whilst just avoiding bad neighbourliness.

Bury St Edmunds combines a grand Tudor house with a Romanesque station. It is most notable for its twin Baroque turrets which once marked the ends of partial overall roofs.

Thurston, predominantly Tudorish, uses a mezzanine to stretch its top storey to railway level.

Needham Market is a Tudor mansion with crenellated towers and flanked by subsidiary entrances in the form of classical pavilions.

Stowmarket is the best of the series and is composed of three Jacobean pavilions. The outer ones are emphasized by octagonal turrets and the centre has an Italianate/classical entrance.

Bury St Edmunds 1979

Bury St Edmunds 1973

Thurston 1973

Above and right
Needham Market 1974

Left and below
Stowmarket 1978

9 Sancton Wood

Sancton Wood worked as architect for the Eastern Counties Railway (GER) and the Syston & Peterborough Railway (MR).

Nobody knows who designed North Woolwich, built in 1847. It has been ascribed to Sir William Tite but it is not really his style. Francis Thompson was busy with the GER at this time and **North Woolwich** could be regarded as an embellished Ely. But the balance of probability is that it is by Wood. Operations have been transferred to a new station alongside and this building is now a museum.

Stamford Town, 1848, is by Wood although the turret is a touch of Tite. It is an imaginative design in Tudor and Gothic to harmonize with the stone-built town it serves.

Luffenham, 1848, is a large Italianate house flanked by two sets of pavilions. The inner ones provide support for an entrance canopy and the outer terminate the platform awning.

Oakham, also 1848, is the best surviving station unambiguously attributed to Wood. The two-storey Italianate building has flanking pavilions terminating the entrance porch supported on Doric pillars. The whole is then equipped with slightly asymmetric single storey pavilions.

North Woolwich 1976

Stamford 1973

**Stamford
1973**

*Right and
below*
**Luffenham
1974**

Oakham
1974

10 Isambard Kingdom Brunel

I. K. Brunel is best remembered as the mechanical and civil engineer of the London & Bristol Railway which quickly evolved into the GWR. In the latter capacity he designed many of the buildings as well. His architecture is, perhaps, notable more for fitness of purpose than for aesthetic appeal but Bradford-on-Avon is attractive enough and the façade at Bristol suitably imposing for a major provincial terminus.

Bristol Temple Meads, 1840, has a splendid collegiate Tudor frontage. The railway was at first floor level in order to clear nearby dock facilities. Entry to the station, which had no concourse across the head of the tracks, was through the archway on the left to a side entrance. Arriving passengers left by an exit, no longer extant, on the right. Inside, Brunel provided an overall roof spanning side platforms and four tracks by using rafters cantilevered from stanchions along the middle of the platforms and tied down by iron bars in the exterior walls. He then added hammer beams and pendants which are structurally pure spoof. The rafters are stiffened with wrought iron bars above and below.

The awkward site at **Bath Spa**, 1841, engenders an asymmetry which is not entirely satisfactory even in Tudor. The awning, which is not, presumably, Brunel's fault, does nothing to help matters.

Culham, 1844, is the smallest surviving station of Brunel's in Tudor style.

More common are similar sized Italianate stations of which **Mortimer**, 1848, is the only complete example. Here Brunel extended the hipped roof on all sides on long modillions to provide shelter below. The matching shelter on the 'down' side (from Paddington via Reading) looks a touch top-heavy in this form. **Pantyffynnon** and **Chepstow**, both 1850, are versions in stone and **Charlbury**, 1853, is in wood. Extended variants in stucco and timber respectively, are Dorchester West and **Torre**, both of 1857. Another good and recently refurbished example can be found at **Bridgend** paired with a glass box entrance block which, for once, is a distinct improvement on the earlier accretion it replaced. Stratford-upon-Avon, 1864, has a posthumous model in brick.

**Bristol Temple Meads
1988**

Bath Spa 1973

Culham
1975

Mortimer
1975

Mortimer 1975

Pantyffynnon 1976

Chepstow 1978

Charlbury 1978

69

Torre 1977

Bridgend 1987

Frome, 1850, has the only remaining overall roof of a kind designed by Brunel and used widely all over the GWR system. The combination of wooden rafters with slim iron tie rods gives the interior a feeling of considerable space. The accompanying buildings were in stone, brick or wood. In accordance with Murphy's well known law, Frome is in timber.

Heyford and **Kidlington**, 1852, illustrate a design used repetitively north of Oxford. They once had all-round awnings adorned with metal animal masks. The sole survivor at Kidlington, a contractors depot in 1978, has now probably vanished. Note the curious provision of a bay window at the end of the building. This is an idiosyncrasy which can often identify a Brunel station.

Frome 1972

Frome 1972

Heyford
1978

Kidlington
1978

Kidlington 1978

St Germans and **Lostwithiel**, both 1859, are West Country variants of the Heyford type having gabled, instead of hipped, roofs but incorporating the same central recessed shelter on the platform side.

Bradford-on-Avon, 1858, is an individual Tudor design with the characteristic end bay window and is, perhaps, Brunel's most charming. An extended, less attractive version, on the same line, was **Trowbridge**, of the same year. Owing to decay it has had to be replaced in the railway-post-modern style.

St Germans 1977

Lostwithiel 1977

Above and left
Bradford-on-Avon 1978

Trowbridge 1972

11 Sir William Tite

Tite was a Victorian of wide abilities in addition to being one of the era's most important architects. His extensive railway work was completed before he received his knighthood and formed only the lesser part of his architectural achievement. Most of his stations are Tudor in form or flavour but the early ones for the London & Southampton Railway, soon to become the LSWR, are classical.

Micheldever, 1840, is a classical/neo-Georgian villa faced with knapped flint and has an all-round awning. **Winchester**, of the same year, has been much altered over the years. Only the central part of the upper storey is as Tite intended.

Dorchester South came later, in 1847, and was originally the terminus of the Southampton & Dorchester Railway. Pilasters and cornice are applied to a single storey building. The central awning was a later addition. For many years, after the line was extended to the GWR line to Weymouth, 'up' trains had to reverse into the terminal platform. Later a platform was provided on the through line. Recently, under a swap agreement with the local brewery, the now remote building has been demolished and replaced by a new one on the platform. Its form recalls Brunel's Mortimer but only the churlish would complain that it is slightly off its right railway.

Micheldever 1973

Winchester 1980

Dorchester South 1977

Later in the 1840s Tite turned his attention to the North. **Lancaster Castle**, 1846, is in fairly large scale Tudor and has survived electrification. At the southern end is a square tower surmounted by a pyramidal roofed turret. The northern end is in more domestic style. **Perth** followed in 1847, built jointly for the CR, HR and NBR. The illustration shows Tite's nicely detailed frontage, with Tudor doorway and oriel window. The octagonal turret was something of a Tite trademark. Since Tite's day the station has been extensively altered and the through platforms are now in front of his façade.

Carlisle Citadel, 1848, is the most impressive of Tite's Tudor stations. The buttressed Gothic entrance has a frieze carrying the arms of the railways for whom it was jointly built (Lancaster & Carlisle Railway, LNWR and Caledonian Railway) in garters. The frontage is balanced by a bay-windowed pavilion and the roof enlivened with a row of dormers. Above these, peering over the roof as it were, are the peaks of the ridge and furrow overall roof within. The clock tower is topped off by a lantern turret.

The Lancaster & Carlisle's **Penrith**, also 1848, is on a more domestic scale, its principal feature being a superior Tudor window for the booking hall.

The remaining stations were all for the LSWR. **Hampton Court**, 1849, is correctly planned but somehow lacks appeal, particularly now that its central entrance has been mutilated and replaced. Tite may have had octagonal chimneys at the apexes of the Jacobean gables which might have helped. **Windsor & Eton Riverside**, partly to serve a more active Royal palace, is much more successful. A buttressed Gothic entrance admits the traveller to a booking hall lit by another superior window. The buttressing is carried along the side wall pierced by a series of large doors to facilitate the entraining of cavalry. This wall also carries built-in graffiti to the Queen and her consort. Beyond is the Royal entrance and waiting room above which Tite placed his Turret. This is supposed to have been used by station staff to gain advanced notice of the approach of Royalty.

Right and below
Lancaster 1984

Perth 1983

Carlisle 1972

Carlisle 1979

Penrith 1976

Hampton Court 1975

Left and above **Windsor & Eton Riverside 1988**

Whitchurch (Hants), 1854, returned to the Micheldever style and was given a classical entrance.

The North Devon Railway forms the LSWR route to Barnstaple, now the only one. In 1854 it built a series of small stations by Tite. **Eggesford** is near symmetrical but has appendages. **King's Nympton**, once known as South Molton Road, is an asymmetrical version with an integral platform shelter and is, perhaps, the most pleasing of the family. One suspects that **Portsmouth Arms** is not by Tite at all. Although in freestone, like the others, its style is more that of the turn of the century. **Umberleigh** hugs the ground and is similar to Morchard Road. Lapford is a less picturesque variant. **Barnstaple**, formerly Barnstaple Junction, is the largest building of the series and is a bit gaunt compared with the others.

**Whitchurch
1977**

**Eggesford
1977**

**King's
Nympton
1977**

Portsmouth Arms 1977

Umberleigh 1977

Barnstaple 1977

In 1859 and 1860 Tite designed a series of stations for the LSWR in the twin pavilion form used by many companies in the latter half of the century. This provides, generally, the booking hall in the linking section, a house for the station master in the larger pavilion and other facilities, such as waiting room, porters room, etc., in the smaller. Tite's were distinguished by steeply pitched roofs and, in many cases, by the house having three storeys. **Godalming** and **Petersfield** are probably Tite's work and are on the Portsmouth direct line. For **Gillingham** and **Sherborne** on the Exeter line Tite shares the kudos with his partner, E. N. Clifton. **Crewkerne, Axminster** and **Whimple** are also on the Exeter line. Axminster has suffered emasculation of its chimneys.

Godalming 1974

Petersfield 1978

Gillingham 1977

**Sherborne
1978**

**Crewkerne
1977**

**Axminster
1977**

Whimple 1977

12 William Tress

William Tress was one of Tite's pupils and in the early 1850s he designed a series of stations for the SER. None is large but most have considerable charm.

Ham Street & Orlestone, **Appledore**, **Rye** and **Winchelsea**, all 1851, are on the Ashford to Hastings line by which the SER first reached Hastings. Rye, Italianate with a loggia entrance, but also having a classical layout with pilastered quoins, looks equally well from public and platform sides – a rare achievement. The others have not been specifically attributed to Tress but, given their location and date, are probably his. Appledore has much in common with Wadhurst. Ham Street and Winchelsea are similar but have no other counterparts on the SER.

Ham Street & Orlestone 1975

Appledore 1975

Right and below
Rye 1975

Winchelsea 1975

Tress's other stations were built in 1852 on the Hastings direct line south from Tunbridge Wells. **Frant** and **Etchingham** are Tudor and apart from the platform canopies are unaltered. The remainder are Italianate. **Wadhurst** and **Stonegate** have been added to on the left. **Robertsbridge** once had belfried chimneys and has been simplified. Although the brickwork is uncommonly well integrated, it is difficult to imagine that the right hand building at **St Leonards Warrior Square** formed part of Tress's design. Without it the balance is near perfect. Missing from this series is West St Leonards, not by Tress, built in cutting, entered via a standard SER clapboard building at street level and recently remodelled.

Frant 1971

Wadhurst 1971

Stonegate 1975

**Etchingham
1974**

**Robertsbridge
1974**

**St Leonards
Warrior
Square
1975**

13 W. N. Ashbee

W. N. Ashbee is not, strictly, an early railway architect because he worked late in the Century. But the number of fine buildings to his credit justifies his inclusion here. He joined the GER engineering department in 1874 and became head of the architectural department from 1883 to 1916. His largest work was the East side suburban station at Liverpool Street, now completely gone and rebuilt under commercial development, but his finest is the rebuilt Norwich Thorpe.

Hertford East, 1888, can perhaps best be classified as corporate Domestic Revival but it has a good deal of Baroque embellishment. Its front porte-cochère, now roofless, has an affinity with that at Norwich.

As would be expected, all the GER's domestic revival stations were built by or under Ashbee. **Southend Vic-** toria is the largest and received a wooden porte-cochère.

Wolferton, 1890s, was a special station for very special passengers being built mainly to serve the Royal estate at Sandringham. Latterly it has been a private museum. The lanterns, once for oil lamps, on fine barley sugar columns, incorporate the Royal Arms in the frieze and have coronets for chimneys.

Colchester, 1896, anticipates Edwardian Baroque and even some features of the 1920s but still has, with its cupolas, something of a revival air. Its charms cannot be glimpsed, or even imagined, from the train.

Felixstowe, 1898, has a glazed lantern and is a seaside terminus in true revival style. The building is no longer in railway use. The concourse was a small replica of that at Norwich.

Hertford East 1977

Southend Victoria 1976

Wolferton 1979

Wolferton 1979

Colchester 1976

Felixstowe 1983

Wolferton 1979

III Company Architectural Styles and Details

Some railways, like the NER, were quick to adopt company styles in building and even stock designs. The employment of a single architect over a wide area tended to produce this as a result. Smaller railways each had their own ideas and perhaps employed an architect for their headquarters station and had the local builder run up something suitable for the others. Or, indeed, very little in the way of buildings was provided at all until such time as revenue would permit the necessary expenditure. By the second half of the 19th century most smaller railways had amalgamated into or had been swallowed up by larger companies and these would begin to appreciate the advantages of a corporate image and the economies of standard designs when new or rebuilt stations were required. The later railways, constructed in the last quarter of the century, used standard buildings, almost exclusively, from the outset.

By the end of the century company acronyms were to be found incorporated in buildings and, especially, in foundrywork details. Relatively few examples survived into the 1970s.

The decorative valancing to platform awnings was executed in almost as much variety as the iron brackets involved in their support. Although sometimes finished to the whim of the local joiner, several designs can be found which can unambiguously be associated with particular companies. Here, again, survivals are rapidly diminishing, for in the last decade general policy seems to have been rather to demolish than to maintain those awnings in need of repair.

1 South Eastern Railway

One early standard design of building used by the SER in large numbers was in 'Kentish clapboard', a superior kind of weatherboarding. They were not all identical but were closely similar and clearly formed a company style. They were gratifyingly cheap to build and, rising from a brick plinth to keep their feet dry, have lasted remarkably well. More have been lost to fire or obsolescence than to decay. **Pluckley**, 1842, is typical. The most presentable survivor is **East Farleigh**, 1844. It retains early chimneys and is enhanced with shelters over the doorways. The most extraordinary is Earley, 1863. Here the wooden building has been built on top of a brick ground floor to form the upper storey of a two-storey building.

The SER used a characteristic awning valance with vertical boards alternately having semi-circular extensions and cut-outs. The extended boards have an attenuated fleur-de-lys perforation or, sometimes, a trefoil one. Some have a tiny circular hole below. In some cases the upper part of the valance formed a frieze punctuated with little roundels. The roundels have nearly all disappeared even where the rest survives. **Coulsdon South**, 1889, provides an example. **Yalding**, 1844, shows the kind of pent-roofed shelter often provided on the 'other' platform, ie the one not containing the main building.

High Brooms, 1893, is not a stock design but, on the contrary, is an individual work by William Barnsley Hughes of Southborough. It is, appropriately for the date, Domestic Revival, but of particular interest is the Roman window over the entrance. This was the first use of this feature on the SER and it appeared later at other SER and SR stations, Margate and Hastings, for example.

Pluckley 1976

East Farleigh
1975

Coulsdon
South
1979

Yalding
1975

2 London, Chatham & Dover Railway

The LCDR was too poor to spend much on architecture and what little money it had it preferred to use fighting the SER. Few of its bespoke designs survive unaltered but two standard forms can still be found.

The earlier form was linked pavilions in which the smaller was even lower than the linking section and almost detached from it. **Farningham Road**, 1860 and **Shepherd's Well**, 1861, are the best examples. Others have been more or less altered. Even these show variation, Farningham Road having its house in line with the railway.

The other design made much use of polychrome brickwork and had openings headed by two-centred arches. **Penge East**, 1863, lately cleansed of a century of grime, can be regarded as the archetype with more convention-al unequal pavilions. Sevenoaks, **Bat & Ball**, 1862, is a mirror version and slightly less colourful. **Herne Hill**, also of 1862, is a one-off design to cater for an embanked railway, but if conforms closely to the colour scheme and the window design. A fragment inside Brixton shows that this station too was in the same idiom. The station pub across the road is labelled as built in 1885 and is called 'The Railway'. It is in a tolerable imitation of the same style.

In the 1880s a variant was repeated on the line from Maidstone to Ashford. Both layout and colour scheme are slightly different but the family likeness is apparent. **Bearstead**, 1884, is typical. Hollingbourne, Harrietsham, Lenham and Charing are similar.

Farningham Road 1980

Shepherd's Well 1975

Penge East 1979

Bat & Ball 1974

Herne Hill 1975

Bearstead 1975

3 London, Brighton & South Coast Railway

In its early days the LBSCR had the services of David Mocatta as its architect but very little of his station work survives. The major fragment forms part of the frontage at Brighton station. In the 1860s the company tended to build small families of stations having a common style rather than a standard plan. One such family comprises Battersea Park, **Denmark Hill** (p. 2) and Peckham Rye, the latter somewhat disfigured and, perhaps fortunately, hidden behind modern shop development. Leatherhead, Groombridge and Tunbridge Wells West have been described as another set. They are distinctly less coherent but share polychrome brickwork and each has a turret or tower.

Later in the decade the first really standard form emerged and was built in quite large numbers. **Ockley & Capel**, 1867, and **Buxted** of the following year typify the stations built on the Horsham and Edenbridge and Buxted lines. They are of the conventional unequal-pavilion-with-linking-block design.

Ockley & Capel 1979

Buxted 1975

In the 1880s, T. H. Myres designed a series of stations used widely on the minor lines of East and West Sussex. Most are now tile-hung but many were originally half-timbered and pargeted as at Cocking, 1881. **Sheffield Park**, 1882, now the headquarters of the Bluebell Railway, is typical. The minor pavilion is dispensed with and the house slightly extended to contain the booking office adjacent to the single-storey section entered via a decorative porch. Most survivors are now out of railway use. **Cocking** had its first floor meticulously extended over the single-storey section. Note the little flower motif incised in the plaster. It can also be found at **Ardingly** and a smaller version is used in the earlier keystones of the window heads at Battersea Park and Portsmouth & Southsea. The chimneys anticipate the decorative effects of the Domestic Revival by ten years but are more delicate.

The larger stations on the coastal line westward from Brighton of the 1880s form another family in an Italianate villa style. They are, perhaps, a development of the old building at **Hove**, 1865, itself an improved version of Arundel of 1863. Hove is a twin pavilion building with small extensions at either end. **Portslade & West Hove**, 1881, with an extended central link, is clearly, the best of the series. **West Worthing**, 1889, had a closer similarity to Hove but was enhanced by an entrance at the head of a stone staircase. **Shoreham-by-Sea** 1892, shows an interesting single storey variant. Other examples are at Brighton London Road and, less attractively, the intermediate building at Polegate. Polegate was opened on the site of the present station but was moved in 1889 to take in the line from Hailsham to Eastbourne.

Sheffield Park 1977

Cocking 1982

Ardingly 1977

Hove 1975

Portslade & West Hove 1975

West Worthing 1975

Shoreham-by-Sea 1975

Towards the end of the century the railway rebuilt several stations featuring a lantern to give top lighting to the booking hall. **Lewes**, 1889, and **Bexhill Central**, 1901, are good examples. Eastbourne, something of an architectural sampler – the unkind might say hotchpotch – has one over the concourse. East Croydon once had one and the associated wooden ceiling that supported it could be seen inside.

About the same time a standard pattern of awning valance was introduced which can still be found quite widely. **Pulborough**, 1900, is a good example. The GER used something similar at Gidea Park but here the essential 'double keyhole' perforations are omitted.

Lewes 1974

Bexhill Central 1975

Pulborough 1975

4 London & South Western Railway

An early standard station building used by the LSWR comprised a central Italianate block flanked by lean-to single storey pavilions with hipped roofs. **Witley** and **Rowland's Castle**, both 1859, are on the Portsmouth direct line and others can be found at Liphook and Haslemere.

Until about 1860 much LSWR architecture was attributable to Sir William Tite and this design also may owe something to his work. Norbiton and Kew Gardens, of 1869, are effectively, extended versions with a central block of five bays under a hipped roof.

Witley 1975

Rowland's Castle
1975

Wateringbury 1982

Aylesford 1991

Atherstone 1985

Louth 1982

Huddersfield
1983

Huddersfield
1983

Ashby-de-la-Zouch 1983

Gravesend 1983

Audley End 1984

Cambridge 1984

Chester 1983

Rhyl 1983

Stowmarket 1981

North Woolwich 1986

Bristol Temple Meads 1978

Windsor & Eton Riverside 1982

Perth 1983

Rye 1983

Stonegate 1986

Hertford
East
1983

High
Brooms
1983

Penge East
1980

Petworth 1982. A superior wooden station of 1859. LBSCR.

Reading 1978. GWR Classicism of 1870.

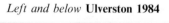

Left and below **Ulverston 1984**

Dumfries 1990

**Taynuilt
1978**

**Kyle of
Lochalsh
1987**

Skipton 1976

Settle 1976

Clare 1981

King's Cross 1982

St. Pancras 1982

Shrewsbury 1983

Manchester
Piccadilly
1982.
The extended
interior of
1881. LNWR.

Glasgow
St. Enoch
1982

Leicester 1981

Bexhill West 1980

Wemyss Bay 1979

Nottingham 1978

Manchester
Victoria
1981

Manchester
Victoria
1981

Stirling 1983

Stirling
1983

Hastings
1988

Cardiff
Central
1987

**Birmingham
International
1978**

**Milton
Keynes
1983**

**Milton
Keynes
1983**

Another standard design was used on the line to Guildford via Effingham Junction. This combines a two-storey house with a single-storey extension to accommodate railway offices. **Clandon** and **Guildford London Road** show the public side and **Claygate**, a mirror version, the railway side. All were built in 1885. Others can be found at Horsley and mirror versions at Oxshott and Cobham.

Worplesdon, 1883, and **Swanwick**, 1889, are the earliest and latest survivors of a third type repeated, with minor variations, at Sway, New Milton and Hinton Admiral. Some, like Worplesdon, have elaborate, Flemish gables and the others more decorative, early Domestic Revival, chimneys. The barrel roofed dormer above the office section is another common feature.

Clandon 1975

Guildford London
Road 1979

Claygate 1979

Worplesdon 1979

Swanwick 1975

5 Great Western Railway

The more impressive station buildings of the GWR tend to be typical more of their time than of the railway. Many, particularly those in Wales, are rebuilds of the 20th century. In the latter part of the 19th century, as the Brunel-inspired designs became outmoded, the railway began to use three designs, each having coherent detailing that gives a strong impression of standardization, even although each individual is slightly different in layout and size.

Stourbridge Town, 1897, has now been demolished to make way for a rail/bus interchange but it well illustrates the features of one series: French pavilion roofs with decorative foundrywork cresting, windows grouped under shallow segmental arches, sometimes polychrome brickwork, and chimneys which, although not exclusive to the railway, are very characteristically GWR. Southall, 1876, was a small version on an overbridge and Langley, 1879, was a two-storey rarity and rather handsome. **Wrexham General**, about 1880, has the roofs but not the other details.

Stourbridge Town 1978

Wrexham General
1973

Hall Green, 1908, shows the second series. The chimneys are similar but the window treatment is different. Note the design of awning valance, widely used on the GWR. Each board is pointed to give a fine sawtooth effect and there is a perforation above the root of each tooth. Occasionally there are two rows of perforations.

The chimneys survived, almost unchanged, into the third series. **Solihull**, 1926, is typical and shows the later window treatment: 'School Board' pattern surmounted by a flat-arched stone or concrete lintel.

The GWR used monogrammed footbridges and platform seats in large numbers. Many of the bridges survive, that at **Hagley**, 1878, being a good specimen. Seats are now much harder to find. The earlier pattern, from about 1900, was at **Wellington**. It has the virtue of looking the same from either direction but some effort is needed to perceive the reversed R as a manuscript G. The later pattern, about 1930, was at **Worcester Shrub Hill**. The solid ground enables the letters to be properly cast on each face.

Hall Green 1978

Solihull 1978

Hagley 1978

6 Lancashire & Yorkshire Railway

Many stations on the LYR were built to individual designs but two families, each incorporating common features, can be identified.

On the line from Wigan to Southport a series of Tudor stations was built in 1854. Gathurst, **Appley Bridge, Burscough Bridge** and **New Lane** are the best of them.

Later in the century, when company styling was in vogue, a much more numerous type was introduced. They had their offices in an entrance block giving access to platforms often above or below street level. Where possible these were island platforms between the tracks. The polychrome entrances were mainly buff brick with red trimmings. The real trademark of this series was the use, at eaves level, of a pattern reminiscent of an heraldic 'label' but presumably based on machicolation very much simplified. Machicolation was the arrangement of corbels bringing the battlements of fortified buildings clear of the walls so that defenders could drop nasty things on attackers from above whilst still protected behind the battlements. **Pendleton** and **Swinton**, both 1887, are typical and show the variation possible. Even at **Walkden,** 1888, the entrance, which might have been a mere hole in the wall, is given the treatment; within was a vintage booking office lit from above by a lantern between the tracks.

Wellington 1988

Worcester Shrub Hill 1985

Appley Bridge 1976

Burscough Bridge 1976

New Lane 1976

**Pendleton
1976**

Swinton 1976

**Walkden
1976**

7 Furness Railway

Examples can be found of two designs of station used repetitively by the FR.

Silverdale, 1857, with its lean-to shelter over the platform, is rather like a junior version of Green's Newcastle & Berwick series of ten years earlier. It was built by the Ulverston & Lancaster Railway. Cark & Cartmel is similar and St Bees has a variant.

Bootle (Cumbria), about 1860, is to a more numerous design. Drigg is similar, whilst some, like Ravenglass, have been more or less altered. Haverthwaite, on the Lakeside branch, now the headquarters of a private railway, is, perhaps, the best example.

The buildings at **Dalton**, 1846, have all been swept away. In 1975 it had a Tudor building in stone, and a ridge-and-furrow glazed awning on the platform. The awning had a metal valance and was supported on spandrel brackets bearing the FR monogram. Like most of the FR brackets, monogrammed or not, they also had little pendants at their outer ends. (A spandrel is the more or less triangular space with one or two curved sides enclosed between two arches of an arcade or between the arch and its enclosing rectangular frame. The shape nicely describes the cast iron brackets used to support awnings and canopies.)

Silverdale 1975

Bootle 1975

Above and right:
Dalton 1975

Ulverston was rebuilt in 1873 by Paley and Austin and has recently been refurbished. It retains its awnings and monogrammed brackets, the latter slightly simpler than those at Dalton. The FR awnings are rather similar to those of the Midland Railway. In the booking hall at Ulverston are some FR seats, probably the only survivors. 'Rustic' seat ends are not uncommon, but the FR design, incorporating a squirrel, the company emblem, with a vine in full fruit for provender, is incomparable.

Ulverston 1984

Ulverston 1984

8 Glasgow & South Western Railway

The G&SWR was the Midland's partner in providing a route from London to Glasgow. No architectural standardization is now apparent, but some of the surviving platform awnings have a distinctly MR flavour.

In 1979 the awnings at **Kilmarnock**, 1878, were supported on brackets bearing the monogram G&SWRCo.

Dumfries, 1859, is nowadays the most impressive station on the railway. Across the road, the Station Hotel is a genuine railway hotel, now, of course, divested to independent ownership.

Troon was rebuilt in 1892 by James Miller mainly in timber. Its awnings are supported by a striking network of iron joists. In 1979 it still sported a vintage platform clock borne on wrought iron brackets.

Kilmarnock 1979

Dumfries 1979

Troon 1979

Troon 1979

9 Caledonian Railway

The largest group of standard buildings on the former Caledonian Railway is in Glasgow and deserves to be better known. The Cathcart Circle service starts and finishes at Glasgow Central and, accordingly, in the long run gets you nowhere. But in the process, this little excursion across the Clyde visits a unique and charming series of suburban stations. All were built in the late 19th century. Authorities variously suggest dates as 1886 or 1894. Each station has a single island platform with access from roads crossing over or under the railway.

The eponymous **Cathcart** and the similar **Pollockshaws East** have entrances from below at either end of the platform. The sole building is on the platform and has booking facilities at one end. The all-round glazed awnings are supported on brackets formed of a wood and iron sandwich whose clasping rivets form a decorative pattern. Further decoration is provided by an infilling of wooden spindles. At either end the peak of the roof of the building extends above the awning to give a gabled hip effect. **Shawlands** has one entry from above, here seen in the distance, and one from below. Mount Florida and Queen's Park are similar but their entries at the plat-

Cathcart 1979

platform ends are both from overbridges. **Maxwell Park** and **Pollockshields West** are two-storey variants, in cutting, and have central entrances via the upper storey from either side of the railway. **Crosshill** was squeezed into a narrow cutting and had to be smaller than standard. It has an entrance only at one end. The other stations on this route, Pollockshields East and Langside, have been unremarkably rebuilt since the last war.

Cathcart 1979

Pollockshaws
East 1979

Shawlands 1979

Maxwell
Park 1979

**Maxwell Park
1979**

**Pollockshields
West 1979**

**Crosshill
1979**

The Callander & Oban Railway became part of the CR and it had built a series of stations in timber on brick plinths – a dour form of Cottage Orné. **Taynuilt**, 1890, is the only survivor and even there the matching shelter, once adorned with antlers, has succumbed to rot. Connel Ferry and Crianlarich Lower were other examples and had lasted until the 1960s. Oban, at the end of the line, was in the same style but much bigger and topped by a clock tower. It is now out of railway use and trains terminate outside.

Lockerbie, 1848, is similar to the former station at Beattock by Sir William Tite but is still operational. In 1979 it had a CR seat with ends appropriately monogrammed and embellished with thistle heads and Arts and Crafts foliage.

Taynuilt 1972

Right and below
Lockerbie 1979

10 North British Railway

The earliest section of the NBR forms part of the East Coast route from London to Edinburgh and beyond, in partnership with the GNR and NER. But standardization of architecture had to wait for the West Highland section of the 1890s.

From Helensburgh Upper to Corrour all the stations have island platforms and most have standard buildings like those at **Garelochhead** and **Tyndrum Upper**, both 1894. The platforms also accommodated the signal boxes. The buildings have been described as in the Swiss chalet style and, indeed, above the brick or stone bases, they are sided with scalloped wooden shingles of Swiss origin. The hipped roofs are sprocketed to give a shallower pitch at the edges. The overhang, also reminiscent of Swiss practice, but equally of Brunel's Mortimer style, provides platform shelter. The end screens are, however, peculiarly Scottish.

**Garelochhead
1979**

 **Tyndrum
Upper
1978**

From Tulloch to Fort William side platforms are used and the buildings were adapted to single-sided form as at Tulloch and **Spean Bridge**. At Fort William itself the line has been cut back to a modern system built station of considerably less charm than the original which stood at the loch side.

On the West Highland Extension Railway to Mallaig side platforms were again used and the buildings, slightly simplified, were finished in cement to match the mass-concrete bridges and viaducts used on this section. **Glenfinnan**, 1902, is the best surviving example of this variant.

**Spean
Bridge
1978**

Glenfinnan 1972

11 Highland Railway

The Highland Railway had its headquarters at Inverness. Its lines were built late enough in the 19th century for the stations to conform to standard designs. In fact four different designs can be identified to which wayside stations were built. The terminal stations were individual although Thurso and Wick were almost identical, each having a small wooden overall roof just long enough to shelter the engine and first coach of arriving trains. **Kyle of Lochalsh** had an island platform with a central, low wooden building whose bays are punctuated by little pilasters. The main station at Inverness has a triangular track layout and two divergent sets of platforms for trains to the north and south separated by a pleasant, open brick arcade.

The earliest standard design is found on the main line north from Inverness. **Fearn**, 1864, Ardgay (once Bonar Bridge) and Alness are all similar and consist of a central, stone-built house flanked by single storey wings. On the platform side is a lean-to, colonnaded shelter.

Left and below
Fearn 1978

The next type is further north on the same line. **Rogart**, about 1868, is typical, a low-built Highland cottage, just the thing to fit snugly into a northern winter. **Lairg**, of the same era, is similar but placed a little away from the platform. Invershin also is, or was, similar, looking rather forlorn in the 1970s.

The Skye Railway, west from Dingwall, used a design with a three-gabled elevation. **Garve** and **Achnasheen**, both 1870, show the form and Strathcarron is another.

At Achnasheen, now the principal crossing place for trains, the platform is shared with the station hotel. The exaggerated space between the lines of the passing loops to be seen at Garve, about 9 feet instead of the normal 'six foot way', commemorates one of the original objectives of this line – a two-way traffic in fishing vessels from the North Sea to the Irish Sea avoiding the sea passage via the Pentland Firth and Cape Wrath. No such traffic was ever offered.

Rogart 1978

Lairg 1978

Garve 1973

Achnasheen 1978

In the 1880s and 1890s many stations were rebuilt on the southern main lines of the HR in the form of twin single-storey pavilions with a linking section extended to form a colonnaded platform shelter. The public side was subject to some variation. **Pitlochry**, 1890, is the finest example and, like Nairn, has an attractive timber building with a gambrel roof on the minor platform. Other stations which are simplified examples of the same design are Newtonmore, 1893, Tain, Brora and the former Moy. **Carrbridge** is a timber version.

Although scarcely a standard design, **Golspie**, 1868, and **Helmsdale**, about 1872, have some similarities as did also The Mound. But Golspie at least earns a place in this book as perhaps the most attractive small wayside station in Great Britain.

Pitlochry 1984

Pitlochry 1973

Pitlochry 1973

Carrbridge 1973

Golspie 1973

Helmsdale 1978

12 North Eastern Railway

Much NER architecture has already been described in connection with its architects, each of whom practised a good deal of standardisation. One design used during Bell's tenure of office, but not specifically attributed to him, can be seen on the former Swinton & Nottingly Railway (MR and NER joint). In each case a two-storey building of four to seven bays is flanked by symmetrical single-storey pavilions provided with bay windows on the railway side. The theme is reflected in the shelter on the subsidiary platform. **Pontefract Baghill**, **Bolton-on-Dearne**

and **Moorthorpe**, all 1879, are illustrated here but may not all survive, being on a line now unstaffed. Chester-le-Street is similar and Goole seems to have been, although one pavilion has now given way to a modern style entrance block.

The NER made some use of monogrammed spandrel brackets. The one shown is at **Hartlepool**, 1880, and there are others at Middlesbrough. In the absence of the monogram a quatrefoil motif was often used.

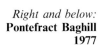

Right and below:
**Pontefract Baghill
1977**

Bolton-on-Dearne 1977

**Hartlepool
1978**

13 Great Northern Railway

The GNR used one or two standard designs but most of its stations were individuals. The company style, however, was almost exclusively Italianate, very freely treated and not really enhanced by being almost always done in buff brick. Royston, now rebuilt in Network SouthEast style, looked for all the world as though the bricklayer had made it up on the spot as he went along.

Sandy and **Newark Northgate**, both about 1850, are on the main line to the North, like Welwyn and Wood Green already described. Sandy is an almost conventional twin-pavilion with its larger one extended. Newark on a single storey is a rare approximation to symmetry.

Retford, 1851, and **Grantham**, also on the main line, are more basic Victorian than Italianate. Their platform awnings are supported on enormously extended spandrel brackets, exclusive to the GNR. Others can be found at Nottingham London Road, now goods only.

**Sandy
1977**

**Newark
Northgate
1973**

Retford 1978

In Lincolnshire GNR stations made much use of three-storey towers. **Woodhall Junction**, 1848, is similar to others at Tattershall and Bardney. None of these is now rail-connected and they may not survive.

The rambling coherence of **Spalding**, 1848, shows GNR Italianate at its very best. Note the 'Venetian' window nicely counterpointed by a triptyque on the ground floor.

Baldock and Meldreth, both about 1851, are on the Cambridge line, known to the railway as the Shepreth branch.

Baldock had so far survived being 'Networked' and, since the line here is on an embankment, presents a two-storey aspect to the public. **Meldreth** shows how a station almost completely devoid of formal Italianate features can nevertheless unmistakably be recognised as GNR Italianate.

Leadenham, 1876, now without rails and in private hands, shows another standard design used in Lincolnshire. It was later repeated many times on the joint line (GNR & GER), now closed, from March to Spalding. **Cowbit**, 1882, is typical.

Woodhall Junction
1974

Spalding 1973

Baldock 1977

Meldreth 1977

Leadenham 1975

Cowbit 1980

14 Midland Railway

The Midland Railway very quickly identified itself at its smaller stations by the use of highly decorative barge boards. The practice was still in vogue when the Settle and Carlisle railway was built in 1875. **Thurgarton**, 1846, a charming essay in railway Tudor, has no less than three typical patterns of barge board.

Another common feature was the use of glazed ridge-and-furrow platform awnings, usually supported by fancy cast iron-work. In the 1970s **Melton Mowbray** still had some good awnings dating from 1860. (The station was built in 1840.) The awnings at Loughborough have suffered over the years. Kettering will, one hopes, be more fortunate.

Standard buildings were the fashion by the time the MR built its own route into London from Bedford. Two designs were used but only one has survived electrification. **Harlington**, 1867, is the best example. Others are to be found at Flitwick and Leagrave.

Thurgarton 1977

Right and below
Melton Mowbray 1974

Harlington 1976

In the last quarter of the 19th century the railway made extensive use of logos consisting of its heraldic beast, the wyvern, or a monogrammatic **MR**. The wyvern is similar to a dragon but has only one pair of legs. It mostly appeared in cast iron work while the MR would be in stone, but Hellifield had both in iron and Sheffield both in stone. **Keighley**, 1876, has its entrance building on a bridge spanning the railway and has a characteristic awning to the street supported by brackets incorporating the wyvern. Another excellent MR awning appears on each platform at **Skipton**, 1876, which has a bespoke vernacular building in stone.

The Settle and Carlisle line was built by the MR to complete its own independent route to Scotland by which it could compete with the East Coast and West Coast routes. As such it can never have made a profit and, by financial criteria, should never have been built. All the stations on the line date from 1875 or thereabouts and are a formidable exercise in standardization. There are three common designs and two oddities.

Above and right: **Keighley 1976**

Left and below
Skipton 1976

The smallest standard form is typified by **Newbiggin** which, although a bit forlorn, retains its fancy glazing. The platform elevation has two pavilion gables decorated with quatrefoils and carrying open fretted bargeboards. The public side has a single centrally placed gable opposite the entrance from the platform. This alternate arrangement of gables, front and rear, is common to all three designs. At one end is a lower extension, which is omitted at Horton-in-Ribblesdale. Other stations to this design are at Little Salkeld, Ormside, Dent and **Hawes**.

Hawes is at the end of a branch from Garsdale (Hawes Junction) which made an end-on junction with the NER line from Northallerton.

The intermediately sized standard has low extensions at both ends, carries typically MR 'wavy gables' as seen at Thurgarton, and has trefoil ornaments in the gables on the platform side. The windows are mullioned into three sections. **Langwathby** is probably the best example. Others are Scotby, Cumwhinton, Armathwaite and Lazonby.

Newbiggin 1988

Hawes 1981

Langwathby 1981

The largest design of the series, also with wavy gables and trefoils, has an enlarged extension on the left of the platform elevation carrying a third, smaller, gable. **Appleby** is easily the best example, and indeed in recent years, the best maintained station on the line. Others to this pattern are Kirkby Stephen West and **Settle.**

Many stations have a shelter on the subsidiary platform like that shown at Appleby. A similar building occupies the 'down' platform at Garsdale, which, like Culgaith, is a deviant and not of the family. At Cotehill and Crosby Garrett only station houses survive. Today only Settle, Horton and Appleby are unambiguously in railway use, most of the others being in independent occupation. Many buildings have lost some or all of their original bargeboards and a few have been structurally altered.

Appleby 1988

Left and below:
Appleby 1988

15 Manchester, Sheffield & Lincolnshire Railway

Many of the early stations of the MSLR were classical or Tudor individuals. Some standardization was apparent in the 1850s as at Appleby (Lincs) and Elsham, the latter now demolished, but in the 1870s and 1880s several stations were built in a standard two-pavilion-and-linking-block form.

Conisborough, 1884, like the earlier Dinting, is distinguished by an angular arcade to support the overshot roof making a platform shelter between the pavilions. The bargeboards are pierced with trefoils and trefoil designs also appear over the windows of the smaller pavilions. A matching shelter serves the minor platform.

Conisborough 1976

Right and below:
Conisborough 1976

Woodhouse, about 1884, had a segmental arched arcade and its wavy bargeboards evoke the MR. Wath Central, Habrough and Kiveton Park were similar while Shireoaks was a close variant.

The LYR branch line from Huddersfield made a junction with the MSLR at **Penistone** which, in 1971, had the only remaining MSLR monogrammed brackets. They were still there in 1988 by which time the main platforms for the Manchester direction had been dismantled.

Woodhouse 1977

Penistone 1971

16 Cheshire Lines Committee Railway

The CLC was a railway jointly owned by the MSLR, the GNR and the MR. Three standard designs of station can be identified, two of them closely based on MSLR practice. Other stations, mainly those opened by the Manchester South Junction & Altrincham Railway, were one-off designs.

Ashley, 1863, is on the line continuing from Altrincham towards Chester. It is remarkably similar to Appleby and Elsham on the MSLR built some ten years earlier. **Plumley**, also 1863, is basically the same as Ashley but here part of the platform shelter has been enclosed to form an extended booking office. Mobberley and Lostock Gralam are similar.

At the Chester end of the line **Delamere**, 1870, Greenbank, Cuddington and Mouldsworth are to a design not to be found on the MSLR.

Ashley 1977

Plumley 1977

142

Delamere 1976

Sankey 1976

The stations on the line from Manchester to Liverpool were to a design very similar to that used by the MSLR at Dinting, etc. They were distinguished by a platform shelter between the pavilions nicely finished with a cast-iron segmental arcade and, above all, by a uniquely fantastic variety of bargeboards on the gables. There are no less than five designs of bargeboard, if one includes those of the shelter on the minor platform, and they were repeated at every station. **Sankey** and **Widnes North**, 1873, are typical. The major pavilion has trefoil perforations on the railway side, rather like those of the MSLR, but more closely spaced to give a skeletal effect. The public side has quatrefoil perforations. The smaller pavilion duplicates the trefoil design on its public side but on the railway side the bargeboards have a truly lace-work effect. The minor end gable and the ends of the subsidiary platform shelters have different, simpler, designs. One or two places, like **Flixton**, 1873, have an additional cross member on the major gable and a few have a decorative, if non-working, drinking fountain.

Sankey 1976

Widnes North 1976

Sankey 1976

Urmston, Irlam, Glazebrook, Padgate and Hough Green are all to the same design but not all have survived with a complete set of bargeboards. Many have lost the minor platform shelter completely and the chimneys may be truncated or removed. Irlam has a vaguely inside-out feeling because it is a mirror version slightly removed from the tracks by an over-wide platform. At **Hunt's Cross**, 1879, the railway was in cutting and a different building was needed; but the fenestration conformed to the company pattern. **Cressington**, 1873, was another variant where the railway was in cutting but still the windows and bargeboards proclaimed 'CLC'.

Aigburth and St Michaels, also on this route, were built earlier, in 1864, by the Garston & Liverpool Railway. They are in a kind of railway Italianate and are clearly not part of the series.

Flixton 1976

Hunt's Cross 1976

Right and below
Cressington 1980

17 Cambrian Railways

The surviving lines of the former Cambrian Railways are all those running west of a point a few miles east of Welshpool on the route from Shrewsbury. They traverse mid-Wales and the coastal route from Aberystwyth to Pwllheli.

Two rather similar designs of station survive in significant numbers. One is exemplified by **Llanbrynmair**, Carno and the operational Caersws which is a mirror version. The house portion has decorative pierced bargeboards, Cottage Orné fashion, and ashlar facings to the doors and windows. A single-storey extension has its roof overshot to form a platform shelter. The other group of stations shares this feature but the house part is less elaborate, although it has a bay window to the platform. **Llwyngwril** is one of the best of this type. Others are at Dyffryn Ardudwy, Harlech, Penrhyndeudraeth and, minus the bay window, Talsarnau. All date from 1867.

Llanbrynmair 1976

Llwyngwril 1976

18 Great Eastern Railway

As we have seen Thompson had introduced a degree of standardization of stations on the constituent railways of the GER from very early days. The company continued with a variety of standard designs for the remainder of the 19th century.

Long Melford, 1865, shows the GER version of the two-pavilions-with-linking-block design which was enlivened by simulated rustication in the brickwork of the quoins. A matching shelter on the subsidiary platform echoed that fronting the link of the main building. Haverhill and

Lavenham, among many others now gone, were similar. **Clare** survives as the headquarters of a country park. **Ongar**, also 1865 is the best preserved in railway use and others can be found on the same line, now part of London Transport. Smaller stations of the type omitted the smaller pavilion, eg North Weald. Other variants, like **Sudbury**, 1865, had added accommodation over the linking section. Marks Tey, now demolished, was similar and Braintree is a less well integrated example.

Long
Melford
1979

Right and below
Long Melford 1979

Ongar 1977

Sudbury 1977

Wickford, Rayleigh, and Hockley, all 1889, show Domestic Revival standardisation on the Southend line, with and without a station house.

Seven Kings, Goodmayes and Chadwell Heath, about 1900, all have entrances on overbridges from which stairs lead down to the platforms. The style is a kind of neo-Georgian used for corporate buildings contemporaneously with Domestic Revival.

Bruce Grove, about 1870, has the kind of ridge and furrow awning with dragon's teeth valancing that was widely used in the suburban area. Lately many examples have had their teeth sawn off to a horizontal line, or the awning has been completely removed, with Ipswich being depicted before such treatment.

Even more widely used was a frilly valancing edging a flat awning shown here at Woodham Ferrers, 1889. There are or were more examples on the Cambridge line and beyond Norwich.

The GER monogram was sometimes used in the ironwork of seats and spandrel brackets. Two varieties of each, from about the turn of the century, could be found in the 1970s and may still be there.

Wickford 1977

Rayleigh 197

Hockley 1977

Goodmayes 1977

Bruce Grove 1977

Ipswich 1978

Woodham Ferrers 1977

Somerleyton 1976

Alresford
1977

Saxmundham 1974

Hainault 1983

19 London, Tilbury & Southend Railway

The LTSR runs from Fenchurch Street to Southend and Shoeburyness. Its inner suburban stations, apart from Stepney East, lately renamed Limehouse, and Barking are now operated by the District Line of London Transport. Stepney East and Fenchurch Street were built by the London & Blackwall Railway, subsequently assimilated by the GER, which accounts for GER flavoured awnings at these stations.

The original building on the 'up' side of the railway at **Upminster** typifies the standard wayside station of the LTSR (The present entrance, on an overbridge, is undistinguished.) It has some similarities to the two-pavilion type of the LCDR. Similar ones can be found at Ockendon, Dagenham East and **West Horndon**, all 1888. The latter shows the platform elevation and one of two awning valance patterns used by this railway. This one is confusingly similar to some used on the GNR.

**Upminster
1977**

West Horndon 1977

Dagenham Dock, about 1888, shows the other valance, resembling the teeth of an old two-handed cross-cut saw, which is uniquely of the LTSR but not many examples survive. Benfleet and Thorpe Bay are similar but with a pierced frieze.

East Ham was rebuilt in 1902 on an overbridge in a style very characteristic of its time. The same design, now minus chimneys, is at Upton Park.

The exuberantly monogrammed brackets of the LTSR were unexcelled by those of any other company. They remain at several stations on the line but **Westcliff**, 1888, has the largest collection. Fewer stations retain monogrammed seat ends. The four-letter logo provides a balanced design which is also structurally sound, as seen at **Southend Central.**

**Dagenham Dock
1977**

**East Ham
1977**

**Westcliff
1977**

Westcliff 1976

20 North London Railway

The North London Railway proper extended no further west than Primrose Hill and in the east failed to reach Stratford. However, by using other people's railways NLR trains could run between Broad Street, its head-

Southend Central 1983

quarters, and Richmond and North Woolwich. Its line was also once important for routing goods traffic between the major railways.

Broad Street, 1866, was demolished in 1985. One of its more pleasant features was the Italianate staircase on the Eastern side giving access to the high-level platforms. In the 1870s the NLR rebuilt many of its stations. There was no standard design but the style was a consistent monumental Italianate as practised at Broad Street up to cornice level.

Hackney, 1873, has been cleaned up and has lost its porch. Railway functions have been transferred to a new building. In 1977 **Mildmay Park**, 1880, had been out of railway use for many years but still carried its name and that of the railway. **Camden Road**, 1873, was known as Camden Town until 1950. The panels in the balustrade above the cornice can still be seen, under the whitewash, dimly to display 'North London Railway' and 'Camden Town Station'.

Acton Central, 1873, was actually built by the North & South Western Junction railway but its style acknowledged its dedication to NLR services.

Broad Street 1973

Hackney 1977

154

Mildmay Park 1977

Camden Road 1978

Acton Central 1979

IV London Main Line Stations

Surprisingly, the oldest main station building in London is **King's Cross** of 1852. It was the terminus of the GNR and, until St Pancras opened, also the MR. The architect was William Cubitt and he anticipated by some 80 years the functionalism of this century. The twin Roman windows reflect the rooflines of the train sheds within. Only the Italianate clock turret and, perhaps, the rustication of the brickwork around the carriage entrance on the right distinguish it from the Art Deco style of the 1930s.

Inside the two sections are divided by an open arcade of brick which supports the rolled iron ribs of the roofs. These ribs replaced original ones of laminated timber in 1870, East side and 1887, West side. The roofs are very much in the form adopted by William Bell at Hull and Darlington. Their outer ends terminate elegantly in glazed screens.

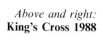
Above and right:
King's Cross 1988

King's Cross 1978

Most of **London Bridge** was rebuilt in 1980/81 and the frontage, never particularly impressive, has been replaced by a bus interchange. The train shed housing most of the terminal platforms was erected by the LBSCR in 1853. The roof is partly supported on cast-iron columns topped by spandrel brackets with similar decoration to that used later by the LCDR at Victoria.

Fenchurch Street is the London terminus that everyone forgets – unless they live near the Thames estuary. It was opened by the London & Blackwall Railway in 1841. They and the GER rebuilt it in 1854 to form the terminus of the London, Tilbury & Southend Railway. The architect was George Berkeley. The renaissance façade has windows separated by brick pilasters and terminated, GER fashion, by rusticated quoins. The segmental pediment corresponded functionally to the curve of a trainshed roof within, now lost to redevelopment. The platforms are at first floor level and were reached via staircases on either side of the booking office. The redevelopment, completed in 1988, has replaced the office by a travel centre on the South side and the stairs by central escalators.

London Bridge 1981

London Bridge 1977

Fenchurch Street 1973

The frontage building at **Paddington**, as so often with terminal stations, is not strictly station but hotel. It was built in a combination of French Renaissance and Baroque by P. C. Hardwick in 1854 at the same time as the rest of the station. The only baroque details now are the figures in the pediment of the central section representing Peace, Plenty, Industry and Science. The remainder, including decorative iron balconies and supporting caryatids, were swept away in 1936 when the GWR 'tidied up' the façade to a state then thought proper. The station itself was built by the GWR's engineer, I. K. Brunel with architectural assistance from his friend, Matthew Digby Wyatt. The trainshed has three semi-elliptic roofs crossed by two transepts and is commonly regarded as the most imposing in Great Britain. A stanchion supports every third rib of the roof in the manner pioneered by Dobson at Newcastle. In 1916 the stanchions had to be renewed to avoid collapse and at that time a fourth bay was added on the North East side. Note Wyatt's decorative treatment of the wall of the station buildings in their traditional place adjoining Platform 1; also his arabesques in iron on the end screen of the centre bay and the cast-iron appliqués to the lower ends of each roof rib. A statue of Brunel sat in the part of the concourse known as The Lawn but more recently he has been moved back to a place near the escalators to the Underground.

Left and below **Paddington. Great Western Royal Hotel 1981**

Paddington 1988 (Three views)

Paddington 1988

Paddington 1985

Cannon Street, 1864, was the City terminus of the SER. Of the original work by E. M. Barry and Sir John Hawkshaw only the twin towers and the Thames bridge remain. The towers used to punctuate the end of a crescent trussed overall roof. This was damaged in the Second World War and later dismantled. The frontage and concourse were disfigured by an office block in the 1960s.

Although railway offices lurked on the ground floor the building at **Charing Cross**, 1864, is nearly all hotel. It was designed by Edward Middleton Barry for the SER as its West End terminus. The style is mainly French Renaissance but the obvious clues of pavilion roofs disappeared when the top storeys were damaged in the war. In 1951 the attic storeys above the cornice were rebuilt incongruously in a Lutyens style. The station clock on the concourse still, improbably, survives despite extensive new developments over the platforms.

Cannon Street 1988

Above and left
Charing Cross 1988

Broad Street, 1865, was designed by William Baker. It was the principal station of the NLR and the company headquarters. It was, accordingly, the biggest and best example of the company's monumental Italianate style, at least up to the cornice; above it had a crown of French pavilion roofs. For 72 years it had been disfigured by a structure on Liverpool Street in front of it, perpetrated by the LNWR. But death is the great healer – the whole lot was demolished in 1985.

Originally the MR had reached London at King's Cross by courtesy of the GNR and the use of its line from Hitchin. Its own belated terminus at **St Pancras** had the train shed completed first in 1868. The designer was W. H. Barlow who had as consultant R. M. Ordish who had worked on the Crystal Palace. The shed spans 240 feet without intermediate support, and is 100 feet high. The outer end has no screen but is finished in an imposing iron lattice. The arches are tied by iron rods passing below the tracks and platforms which are on an undercroft designed to house beer barrels from Burton – an early traffic. The station was built at first floor level because the MR had elected to pass over the Regents Canal just to the north. St Pancras was one of three similar large, single span, train halls. Of the others, Manchester Central, built by the CLC, survives as an exhibition centre; Glasgow St Enoch, of the G&SWR, does not.

Charing Cross 1983

Left and below
Broad Street
1973

St Pancras
1986

St Pancras 1986

St Pancras 1974

The Midland Grand Hotel, forming the frontage of St Pancras, was designed by Sir George Gilbert Scott and added in 1873. He achieved a fantastically detailed, major example of High Victorian Gothic. The frontage of the Western block would not disgrace a cathedral. The main range of the building, terminating in the clock tower, is punctuated by multi-storey oriels and, above the cornice, a roof-scape with a splendid double row of garret dormers topped with Jacobean chimneys. The integrated booking hall, on the traditional 'departure' side, was sympathetically refurbished a few years ago. The wooden booking office, with its linenfold panelling, is outstanding.

Left and below **St Pancras 1988**

St Pancras 1988

The West side of **Liverpool Street** was designed by Edward Wilson and built by the GER in 1875 as its main terminus and offices. The outside, styled in a stodgy Gothic, found few friends and has succumbed to redevelopment. Originally the clock tower had a pyramidal roof which would have improved the balance. The train hall within, in a uniquely free wrought iron Gothic, is altogether splendid and has rightly been preserved within the recent redevelopment. Side aisles flanking twin naves and a transept over the main concourse made it truly a cathedral of iron. Although smaller, it deserves equal rating with Paddington. Indeed, Liverpool Street has lately gained a second, matching transept over a new concourse abutting the inner wall of the hotel. The Gothic theme is continued in the Early English openings in the brick side walls. The Edwardian tea room over the concourse, once the haunt of Sir John Betjeman, has been lost in the extension of the platforms. Most of the frontage to Liverpool Street is formed by the **Great Eastern Hotel**, 1884. It was designed in a Dutch style by Charles Barry, the son of Sir Charles of Palace of Westminster fame.

Liverpool Street 1986

Liverpool Street 1978

Liverpool Street. Great Eastern Hotel 1989

Liverpool Street 1986

Liverpool Street 1974

Liverpool Street 1986

Liverpool Street 1986

The East side of Liverpool Street was built in 1894 by W. N. Ashbee principally for suburban services. The building has recently been lost and the platforms submerged beneath a large new office block. The train hall did not repeat the style of the West side and was of less interest. The concourse had another tea room in use for many years as offices. Above the booking hall windows near the entrance from Bishopsgate were tympana containing carvings in brick of cherubs or putti engaged in a variety of railway tasks. They have been saved and one, at least, has been re-erected, so there is hope for the others. Col. Robert Edis was the architect for the extension of the hotel in 1901 completing the return elevation to Bishopsgate. This section is known as the **Abercorn Rooms**, the GER chairman at the time being Lord Aberconwy.

Liverpool Street. Abercorn Rooms 1986

Marylebone. Great Central Hotel 1986

166

**Marylebone
1981**

**Marylebone
1986**

Edis also designed the Hotel Great Central at **Marylebone**, 1899. The terracotta detailing anticipates the baroque of the following decade and some Norman Shaw influence can be seen in the stripy clock tower. Originally financed independently of the railway, which was strapped for cash, the hotel has for some years been the headquarters building of British Rail, but is now awaiting reconversion to its original purpose. Marylebone, 1899, was the last terminus in London to be opened and could still be the next to close after Broad Street. It was built by the Great Central Railway, as the MSLR now called itself, on the completion of its redundant main line to London. Architectural details for this Flemish style station were by H. W. Braddock. The attractive porte-cochère doubles as a covered way to the rear of the hotel.

The earliest building now at **Victoria** is the adjoining Grosvenor Hotel by J. T. Knowles, built independently in 1861. It was acquired by the LBSCR in the 1890s, incorporated into a rebuild of their part of the station and then leased to an independent hotel company.

Victoria. Grosvenor Hotel 1988

167

Although there is an Italianate flavour below the main cornice the overall style gives one of our best examples of Victorian French Renaissance. Note the garret dormers, the decorative railings and parapets and the Baroque detailing of the windows, complete with faces in roundels.

Sir John Fowler was the engineer to the Victoria Station & Pimlico Railway Company. This was a 'terminals' company, rare in this country, formed specifically to build a station for use by other railways – in this case the LCDR and the LBSCR. The train shed of the LCDR or 'Continental Departures side of the station and the adjoining offices are the only parts surviving from 1862. It ranks after Glasgow Queen Street as the lightest and most pleasant of our Victorian train halls.

In 1908 the LBSCR rebuilt their frontage, the central part, in a timely Baroque of red brick and Portland stone. The designer was Sir Charles Morgan. Another clock in a contemporary facing is inside on the concourse.

Not to be outdone, the South Eastern & Chatham Railway Companies Managing Committee, to give the full name of the jointly run South Eastern and London, Chatham & Dover Railways, rebuilt their frontage, the Eastern side, the following year in white Portland stone. The architect, A. W. Blomfield, incorporated the only caryatids currently in our railway service. Their sexy appearance emphasizes their function as mainly decorative, although they support the broken pediments above. A case of being both engaged and engaging.

Victoria. Grosvenor Hotel 1982

Victoria 1975

Right and below:
Victoria 1988

Victoria 1982

Left and below:
Victoria 1988

The main entrance at **Waterloo** was rebuilt in 1922 by J. R. Scott, the architect of the LSWR. It is in Portland stone and bronze in the form of a triumphal arch commemorating the 1914-1918 war. The style is Imperial Baroque, or, in basic English, embellished stonework with Britannia on top. Flanking the arch are sculptures depicting War and Peace. At the foot of the steps are pylons supporting bronze lamps with L&SWR in roundels between. In an excess of zeal for 'Network SouthEast' styling the bronze has lately been painted over. Inside is a simpler, modern/Baroque arch and nearby is the nicely refurbished 'Windsor Bar', now a travel centre but retaining its redundant former pay-boxes, also lettered LSWR. At the Southern end of the concourse a balancing archway announces the counties served by the LSWR – a reminder of the much more ambitious list of destinations that once adorned the entrances of the former Blackfriars station. At Blackfriars they can now be seen near the ticket barrier. In the tympanum of the arch is a stained glass rendering of the company coat of arms.

The rebuilding of **Euston** was completed in 1968. There was much wailing and gnashing of teeth at the destruction of the Propyleum or 'Doric Arch' which might better have been devoted to the loss of the Great Hall and Boardroom. But the straggling mess of the old station had to go. The new one cowers behind large office blocks and, although it follows the British Rail house style of the time well enough, it scarcely does justice to the country's most important station. Had it been required at a slightly less prestigious site it would be entirely admirable. The inconvenience to travellers of the long trek to the trains within, almost defies belief. Robert Stephenson the engineer of the London & Birmingham Railway stands subdued in the courtyard.

Waterloo 1988
(Three views)

**Waterloo 'Windsor Bar'
1986**

Waterloo 1988

Euston 1981

Euston 1975

Euston 1983

V   Other Noteworthy Stations

This chapter gathers together in chronological order, but otherwise arbitrarily, some architecturally interesting 19th century stations which the organization of this book might otherwise exclude.

Collingham, 1846, is a splendidly elaborate Italianate station by the MR. The pedimented gables at either end seem almost to have been added as an afterthought to the hipped roof which would have been normal. When last seen it was in a state of decay.

As designed by T. K. Penson for the Shrewsbury & Hereford Railway, **Shrewsbury**, 1848, had two storeys. The present ground floor was added in an underpinning operation in 1904. The style is Collegiate Tudor, or Tudor on the grand scale, and incorporates octagonal chimneys, a crenellated parapet and, in the clock tower, a fine oriel window.

The present station at **Bristol Temple Meads** was built in 1865 jointly for the GWR and MR. It was designed by Sir Matthew Digby Wyatt and extended and largely replaced Brunel's earlier London & Bristol station. It is an ebullient Tudor on the outside and mainly Gothic within. The furrows of the external ridge and furrow awning terminate in shields alternately displaying the arms of London and Bristol. Inside, the trusses of the roof spanning the two main platforms reflect the Gothic styling of the entrance foyer. Although not quite the equal of Newcastle or York, the curve of the roof gives it considerable character. The station was given platforms outside the overall roof in 1932-35 and the present booking office, recently refurbished, also dates from that time.

Collingham 1977

Shrewsbury 1983

Bristol Temple Meads 1973

Left and below: **Bristol Temple Meads 1978**

The entrance to **Glasgow Queen Street** cowers beneath new office developments of the 1950s and was given a new look about that time. It is on the western flank of what was the North British Hotel, but the station within has the finest crescent-trussed overall roof in the land. It is by James Carswell for the NBR and was built in 1877. It has an unobstructed span of 250 feet and, weather permitting, has an unequalled air of spaciousness and light. In the north west corner the ends of the principal trusses are supported on stumpy Corinthian columns – a typically Victorian touch. The ends of the hall are unusually well finished in radially glazed screens.

Glasgow Central station, by Sir Robert Rowand Atkinson, was opened by the CR in 1879 and extended by James Miller at the turn of the century. The interior overall roof is held up by lowering, slightly daunting compound gliders. The best bits are outside – the iron and glass porte-cochère and the massive entrance gates.

The main line terminus of the G&SWR at **Glasgow St Enoch** is now long gone but its companion Underground station, 1896, rightly survives, if only as a travel centre. The present station entrance has been integrated with the bus station a little to the south. It is in red sandstone and is a splendid combination of Scottish Baronial and anticipated Edwardian Baroque styles.

Above, right and below:
Glasgow Queen Street 1979

Glasgow Central 1979

Glasgow Central 1979

Glasgow St Enoch,
Underground 1981

Crystal Palace 1975

Until the SER High Level station was closed, **Crystal Palace**, built by the LBSCR in 1875, was known as Crystal Palace Low Level. Shorn of its porte-cochère the Italian/French style exterior is rather gaunt, but the cavernous interior, housing the stairs to the platforms, has some appeal, if only to the devotee, and deserves to be better known.

The North Western Hotel at **Holyhead**, 1880, formed the frontage of the station. From any distance it looked like a naval barracks and few can have regretted its demolition a few years ago. It had a redeeming feature however, in its cantilevered iron and glass porte-cochère, still charming, even without its glazing, in 1976.

Leicester, 1892, can be regarded as the first major MR station to be rebuilt in a programme which bridged the turn of the century. The architect was Charles Trubshaw. The entrance building, largely on a bridge spanning the tracks beneath, is fronted by a long porte-cochère in brick and terracotta surmounted by a pierced parapet punctuated with urns. The beehive and cupola top to the clock turret can also be found on the Midland Hotel at Manchester.

Crystal Palace 1979

Holyhead 1976

Leicester 1986

Derby was the next in the MR series to be rebuilt and was completed in 1894. The classical arcaded porte-cochère was added in 1902. The whole was suitably ambitious for the headquarters and works city of the railway. In 1985 it was completely demolished and only the wyverns round the clock survive to be incorporated in a wall at the far end of the car park. The replacing building, completed in 1988, might be claimed to be more in keeping with the interior which had been rebuilt in concrete some decades earlier.

Wigan Wallgate, 1896, had another late Victorian porte-cochère, this time by the LYR. Contemporary buildings on the platform were replaced by CLASP type in the late 1970s.

Above and right:
Derby 1983

Derby 1971

**Derby
1983**

Wigan Wallgate 1975

VI   Twentieth Century Stations

1 1901 to the Second World War

The first decade of the century saw the building of a number of stations in designs which could equally well have been executed at any earlier time in railway history. Domestic Revival also continued for a few years. But Edwardian exuberance also brought forth stations in a form more nearly Baroque than any in this country before or since. Baroque is a more ornamental form of Classical architecture and, traditionally, more massive. It uses Classical details for decoration rather than structure and elaborates them with added features. Pediments are commonly 'broken', the apex or centre of the base being set back from the rest or even omitted. Sculptural infilling is usual and panels often carry 'swags' or festoons of leaves or flowers in bas-relief. Elevations incorporate curves and in plan a series of curves often replaces straight lines and rectangles, particularly for towers and turrets.

The second decade, inhibited by war, produced only a handful of stations in similar styles. The 1920s saw the first influences of the Modern Movement which, in spite of the economic depression, came to full flower in the 1930s. The Southern Railway, particularly, perhaps vying with or frightened by its neighbour and competitor, the London Underground, built attractive Art Deco stations in great variety. This was the railway's heyday; excursions were a growing business so it is not surprising

that many rebuilt stations were at seaside resorts.

Externally **Edinburgh Waverley** station is just a large hole in the ground. Within the hole it is in the form of a large island platform whose outer faces serve through trains, whilst terminating ones are accommodated in bay platforms at either end. The principal building, in the centre of the island, was rebuilt in 1902 and contains one of the best surviving booking halls in the land. It is in a modest Baroque style and lit from above through decorative iron screens.

Elgin, 1902, was built by the pretentiously named Great North of Scotland Railway. It is the only surviving station in the 'Scottish Baronial' style. It has much in common with English Tudor but is distinguished by crow-stepped gables and conically roofed turrets. Elgin's fine booking hall, lit by a barrel lantern, has been out of use for many years since the Great North's routes were closed and a modern station now operates on the HR's through line.

The Duke of Sutherland was closely concerned in the Caithness Railway and had his own private station at **Dunrobin** to serve his home at Dunrobin Castle when it opened in 1870. The present station, in very rustic Cottage Orné, was a rebuild of 1902 when the HR was in charge. In 1978 it was in use as a store for the Dunrobin estate.

Edinburgh Waverley 1987

Elgin 1972

Elgin 1972

Dunrobin 1978

Bexhill West, 1902, was the South Eastern & Chatham Railway's bid to compete with Bexhill Central, rebuilt by the LBSCR the year before. In Domestic Revival style, topped by a Baroque clock turret, it is at the end of a branch line no longer and functions as a pub and offices.

Bognor was rebuilt by the LBSCR in 1902 in a rambling Revival manner after a fire. On the concourse is a tea room with a contemporary bow front.

In 1903 the CR built **Wemyss Bay** in a whimsical Revival style complete with clock tower. It might almost have been a golf club-house but that it was curved in sympathy with the flower-bedecked concourse within, that connected platforms, booking office and pier.

Bexhill West 1986

Right and below:
Bognor 1978

Wemyss Bay 1972

Wemyss Bay 1972

The MR continued its rebuilding programme in 1904 with **Sheffield**. Charles Trubshaw designed it with a porte-cochère frontage in the manner he had used at Leicester twelve years earlier. This time the building was alongside the railway. Although the building is usually on the 'up' side of a provincial station Sheffield is one of the many exceptions where the pull of the town takes precedence. Note the slightly Baroque features of the arcade, the characteristically MR glass roof and the monograms and wyvern.

Nottingham, designed by A. E. Lambert, was rebuilt in 1904 also. As at Leicester, the façade is porte-cochère and straddles the railway on a bridge. It is Edwardian Baroque in full cry. The clock within, which must have been added in the 1930s, has now disappeared. The booking hall, Baroquely tiled and lit by a barrel lantern, rightly continues in business.

The LBSCR resited **Horley** in 1905. The neo-Georgian building, on an overbridge, still incorporates some LBSCR Domestic Revival features.

Above and right:
Sheffield 1980

184

Right and above
Sheffield 1980

Nottingham 1988

Nottingham 1978
(three views)

Horley 1979

The GWR's main station in Birmingham was Snow Hill. Suburban services in the Wolverhampton direction had bay platforms but for the Stratford and Leamington direction Snow Hill Tunnel was in the way. The platforms were put at the other end of the tunnel at **Moor Street**, 1909, which looked as though it had escaped from the Metropolitan Railway. Services have now been trans-ferred to a new station alongside and to a new Snow Hill.

The LYR gave **Manchester Victoria** a new frontage in 1909. It is by William Dawes in Edwardian Baroque. In 1973, before it was cleaned to pristine condition, it seemed even more vulgarly exuberant. The booking office, extravagant system map and tea room are period pieces.

Birmingham Moor Street 1978

Manchester Victoria 1986

Manchester Victoria 1973

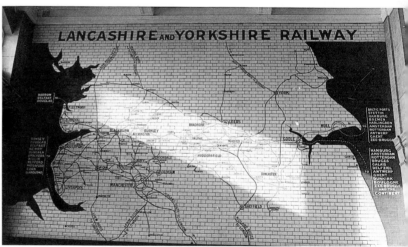

Manchester Victoria 1980

Above and right:
Manchester Victoria 1979

Harrow and Wealdstone, **Hatch End** and **Bushey** were rebuilt by the LNWR when they electrified the line to Watford, in 1911. Gerald Horsley was the designer. They show how Domestic Revival was giving way to truly contemporary design. Note the Norman Shaw touches and the initialled parapet at Harrow, the Baroque swags at Hatch End and, despite the electrification, the weather vane at Bushey.

Stirling was rebuilt by the CR in 1921. James Miller gave it Scottish stepped gables with CR monograms. The ball finials are curious; thistles would have been more usual. The inside is pleasantly light and spacious. The clocks on platforms 2 and 3 have now given way to small, standard ones flanked by television type annunciators.

The South Eastern & Chatham Railway built **Whitstable** in 1915. It has duplicate classical buildings on each side of the line.

Harrow
and
Wealdstone
1978

Hatch End
1978

Bushey 1978

Stirling 1978

Left and below
Stirling 1978

Whitstable & Tankerton 1975

Aberdeen was another wartime building completed in 1916. It was a joint station for the CR and Great North of Scotland Railway by J. A. Parker. Its Baroque detailing somewhat conflicts with its angular form. The building housed a grand top-lit booking hall. During modernisation a few years ago it was given a false ceiling and converted to a travel centre with the ambience of a disco. The travel centre could better have been put on the spacious concourse.

Another CR station by James Miller, **Gleneagles**, 1919, has a traditional entrance and pleasant space within for holiday travellers. The hotel is a mile away and the station has been largely deserted in favour of the private car. Perhaps if a golf course had extended to the station it would have been different.

Walsall was rebuilt by the LNWR in 1922 just in time for the LMSR to take over. The booking hall provided extraordinary grandeur for what became a minor suburban terminus. In 1978 the porte-cochère had been cut off from vehicles by pedestrianisation. Lately, all has gone and the station entrance has been incorporated in a shopping mall.

Right and below
Aberdeen 1976

Gleneagles 1978

**Gleneagles
1978**

Right and below
Walsall 1978

At the end of 1922 the old GWR combined with the smaller railways of South Wales and the Cambrian Railways and became the new GWR. It was the least changed of the 'Big Four'. The new GWR had a taste for classicism when rebuilding in ashlar. **Aberystwyth**, 1924, was one of the first.

Bromley North, 1925, is a terminal essay in new Georgian by the SR. Clock turrets and cupolas were just beginning to be unfashionable.

The SR moved **Margate** a little in 1926. Under a definition no longer fashionable the new building could be described as Baroque. There is a massive central entrance with classical detailing and incorporating the Roman window idea first seen at High Brooms. On either hand symmetrical pavilions are linked to it by arcades in Roman style. In the spandrels are roundels depicting trains, ships and, presumably, the sun.

Ramsgate, also in Thanet, received a new building in the same year. Here Roman windows lit a building showing early, tentative signs of modernism.

Aberystwyth 1976

Bromley North 1975

Margate 1986

Ramsgate 1975

Although the term was not to be coined for another twenty years, **Welwyn Garden City** was a New Town. Its buildings were based on a clearly perceptible class system. The LNER station of 1927 conformed in neighbourly fashion to its high class vicinity. It had a Doric porch on a new Georgian building. Now that the Garden City has been engulfed by a real New Town class distinctions are less obvious. Indeed, by 1990 the building had gone and the station entrance is now integrated in a complete redevelopment of the site.

Byfleet & New Haw, 1927, is a very late hangover from Domestic Revival. It has a SR logo in the ironwork over the doorway. Like many a station serving an embanked railway its appearance comes as a surprise to travellers who only know it from the train.

Welwyn Garden City 1977

Byfleet & New Haw 1979

In architecture generally the 1920s saw a reaction away from Edwardian Baroque. Minor public buildings were erected in a kind of Georgian which formed a stepping stone towards the plainer forms of modernism. Most could equally well have functioned as stations, post offices, labour exchanges or even, if modesty prevailed, banks. Typical of this mood are **Berwick-upon-Tweed**, 1927, and **Clacton**, 1929, both by the LNER and, slightly old fashioned for its day, **Exeter Central**, 1933, by the SR. Berwick is in red sandstone but chiefly noteworthy for carrying beneath its entrance canopy the only set of LNER cast brackets in existence.

Right and below:
**Berwick-upon-Tweed
1976**

Clacton 1977

Exeter Central
1977

Two of the earliest essays into modernism on the SR were **Wimbledon** and **Wimbledon Chase**, both 1929. Perhaps London Transport's extension of the Northern Line to Morden was making its influence felt.

At **Brentwood**, about 1931, the LNER stayed with Revival ideas and even added a Venetian window. Although some platform buildings on the same line received clinical tiling, and Stratford and Maryland had suitably cubist entrances, the LNER seemed to want little to do with modernism.

Wimbledon
1979

Wimbledon
Chase
1979

Brentwood 1977

Close inspection of **Hastings**, 1931, shows it to retain a good deal of classical detailing although its general appearance is a considerable simplification of the earlier Margate and it marks a significant step towards the Art Deco style to come a few years later.

Swansea, 1934, shows more use by the GWR of classically arranged ashlar. The symmetry had to be bent a little to fit the site. **Cardiff**, two years earlier, was in twin-pavilion form with a central clock turret.

J. R. Scott's **Richmond** brought modernism to the SR in 1936. Today it seems typical of contemporary factory architecture. But note the symmetry and the implied classical order in the framing of the windows over the entrance.

Hastings 1976

Swansea 1976

**Richmond
1979**

Falconwood, 1936, and **St Mary Cray**, also of the 1930s, exemplify Art Deco styling on a smaller scale. The generally cubist forms with horizontal glazing and rounded corners are typical.

Charles Holden's work in the modern manner for London Transport about this time has, arguably, yet to be surpassed in any field. His stations have been described as brick boxes with concrete lids but part of his genius was to put the lids well above eye level where the bad weathering qualities of concrete would be invisible. There is a suggestion that he may have had a hand in **Bishopstone**, 1938. This seems doubtful but **Durrington-on-Sea**, 1937, and Bishopstone both have something of the forms he used for the Underground.

Falconwood 1980

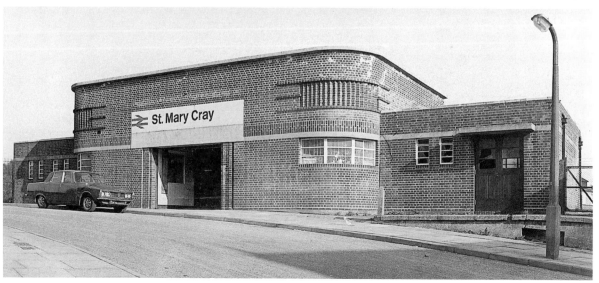

**St Mary
Cray 1979**

**Durrington-on-Sea
1978**

**Bishopstone
1977**

J. R. Scott's **Surbiton**, 1937, was the nearest the SR got to the 'Odeon' style of contemporary cinemas. **Horsham**, 1938, suggests the organ console within and gives the feeling that the windows above the entrance should light up in glowing colours whilst the whole sinks gently into the ground.

The bulk of the town of **Woking** seems to be on the western side of the railway. The station building is on the eastern, 'down' side and is thus wrongly placed on two counts. (The entrance on the 'up' side is just a hole in the wall.) However, it is an excellent specimen of Art Deco with its rounded ends and implicit classical order at the entrance. Although not specifically similar it is nevertheless reminiscent of the contemporary building style of the well known multiple tailor who nowadays shuns the image.

**Surbiton
1979**

**Horsham
1978**

**Woking
1979**

The LMSR built many concrete lidded stations which seemed appropriate at the time but now appear less satisfactory. Perhaps it was because they lacked height and were smaller and cheaper. **Apsley**, 1938, by W. H. Hamlyn is well looked after but many survive less happily and some, in Scotland, have appropriately invited vandalism. **Meols**, 1938, in the Merseyrail area, illustrates the problem. **Hoylake**, of the same year, is still better because of its clerestory but its concrete parts are still too visible.

The SR built a new railway in 1939 and provided J. R.

**Apsley
1979**

**Meols
1976**

**Hoylake
1976**

Scott the opportunity to design a standard station for use on the line to Chessington. Functional entrances, either below or above rail level are combined with reinforced concrete platform shelters of an integrated form. **Malden Manor** and its mirror twin **Tolworth** are rendered and the **Chessingtons (North** and **South)** are in brick. The platforms at Chessington South are in cutting and the consequent absence of superstructure greatly alters the appearance of its perfectly standard entrance.

**Malden
Manor
1979**

**Malden
Manor
1979**

**Tolworth
1979**

**Chessington
North
1979**

Chessington
South
1979

2 Post-War Stations

Banbury, 1959, was one of the first stations to be rebuilt after the Second World War. Its replacement was long overdue and had been deferred owing to the preoccupations of war. It is an individual design with integrated footbridge and lift towers. The entrance is a well-judged mix of pre-fabricated panels, system glazing and in-situ brickwork. The platform structures are in concrete and, ipso facto, less graceful.

The electrification of the line from Crewe to Manchester via Styal was, to some extent, a field trial or pilot scheme for the major project of electrifying the whole West Coast route to Scotland. Many stations were rebuilt in conjunction with the scheme and, to minimize disruption on site, an adaptable prefabricated design was adopted. **Heald Green** and **Burnage**, both 1959, show the early form in which the metal and glass panelled building had a superimposed light-weight roof extended to provide platform shelter. The edging of the roof gave it the appearance of a thick slab. This slab roof became a key feature in British Rail architecture for the next twenty years. Only a few stations received the superimposed roof and the modular building was simplified to the form exemplified at **Styal**, 1960. **Hartford** and **Winsford**, also 1960, are on the main line and show the adaptability of the design.

Banbury 1974

Heald Green 1980

Burnage 1980

Styal 1980

Hartford 1980

Winsford 1980

Manchester Oxford Road was completed in 1960, thirteen years before the antipodean opera house, but it has to be said the latter had been designed and commenced first. Oxford Road is a unique exercise in laminated wood under conoid roofs. It also has shaped wooden shelters on the platforms something like the Chessington ones of 21 years earlier.

Lift towers, something of a feature at Banbury, were given greater prominence at **Broxbourne** and **Harlow Town**, both 1960. Broxbourne has a more conventional modern system built entrance. Harlow, by H. H. Powell, is system building on the grand scale, very fitting for a new town, and incorporates slab roofs. Slightly confusingly for the historian, it is on the site of an earlier station called Burnt Mill and the station now called Harlow Mill was then simply Harlow.

Left and below:
Manchester Oxford Road 1986

Manchester Oxford Road 1982

Broxbourne 1977

Below **Harlow Town 1977**

Ditton, 1961, was Ditton Junction when built and shows the Styal style given a bit of individuality by a clerestory.

In the same year a modern clerestory was applied to the rebuilt **St Helens Central**, formerly St Helens Shaw Street. It could not entirely redeem the sprawling single-storey CLASP building despite its nice vertical glazing.

(CLASP: Consortium of Local Authorities Special Programme. A factory building system to speed the provision of new schools after the war. Now we have too many.)

Chichester, also 1961, is a pleasing individual design by N. G. T. Wikeley. It combines conventional building with modern materials.

Ditton 1980

St Helens Shaw Street 1980

Chichester 1977

Stafford was rebuilt in 1962 in anticipation of the West Coast electrification. It is in reinforced concrete with some prefabrication and has a porte-cochère, a rare feature for a modern station. The building itself, unimpressive from the street, looks more successful from the railway side.

Coventry, 1962, was designed by W. R. Headly of the London Midland Region. The lift towers here are no more prominent than their function demands and the dominant entrance has its slab roof cantilevered over the approach road to give porte-cochère facilities. Inside the high ceiling and large windows combine to provide a splendid booking hall in tune with the rebuilt city it serves.

Left and below:
Stafford 1981

Coventry 1978

Coventry 1978

The entrance building at **Hemel Hempstead**, 1964, also by Headly, is very similar to the platform building at Burnage. But here the roof 'slab' is faced in timber and the system glazing set in in-situ brickwork to give a more domestic, comfortable effect.

About the same time a similar theme was followed at **New Beckenham** but on a smaller scale. **Barrhead** showed an imaginative alternative approach to providing a modern entrance for an elevated railway.

Roof slabs at three levels gave a balanced asymmetry at **Chesterfield**, 1965, but failed to relieve the starkness of the blank walls flanking the entrance.

Hemel Hempstead 1979

New Beckenham 1980

Barrhead
1979

Chesterfield
1977

Ashford, 1965, was an entirely bespoke design based on modern glazed modules. The entrance block is just that and the booking office is placed over the rails flanking the booking hall on the footbridge marked by a small clerestory.

Bletchley, 1966, was another station dominated by lift towers and having a pleasant enough contemporary entrance, but the rest of the frontage looks depressingly like an extended public lavatory. One wonders whether the designers were anticipating Bletchley's eclipse by Milton Keynes.

Northampton, also 1966, is a singleton design. The ridge and furrow glazing of the entrance provides considerable interest and only the churlish would note its resemblance to a factory. The theme is repeated at the ends of the platform structures. Only the awning valances here acknowledge the slab convention.

At Folkestone Central, 1968, N. G. T. Wikeley's use of a slab roof awning over the pavement gives a recognizable British Rail feeling to an entrance that might otherwise have been just a hole in the wall. The logo is featured on a tower that originally carried a clock. Hither Green's subway entrance, of the same period, is similarly thematic on a smaller scale.

Ashford
1980

**Bletchley
1981**

*Right
and below*
**Northampton
1981**

**Folkestone
Central
1981**

Hither Green 1980

Jordanhill, 1970, is characteristic of an extensive family of stations erected in the Glasgow suburban area when it was electrified. The combination of modular glazing with in-situ brick or stone gives full flexibility to suit different sites and the use of opaque panels is happily avoided. A much more welcoming feeling is engendered by the reintroduction of the roof overhang to give shelter on the platform.

The railway needs of **Burton-on-Trent** are much simpler than they used to be and in 1972 it received a much simpler station to match. The now familiar thematic entrance houses booking office and stairhead and is beautifully balanced by the lift tower giving a vertical feature.

On the Southern Region many stations were rebuilt in a prefabricated form using concrete panels to supplement modular glazing. **Kidbrooke**, about 1972, and **East Grinstead**, 1973, show the form. The results were reasonably satisfactory but some stations were more satisfactory than others.

**Jordanhill
1979**

Burton-on-Trent 1974

Kidbrooke 1980

East Grinstead 1979

Maze Hill, 1972, was one of the first of the glass boxes which, in simpler form, were used extensively on the Southern and Eastern Regions. It was a clever design to bring all the functions of a passenger station under one roof and permit minimum staffing. Proliferation made it tedious and it could now be regarded as the railway version of the unacceptable face of modernism by current fashion.

In 1973 **Stevenage** was moved somewhat southward from its original position which did not suit the New Town. The new station is of the 'lift tower' type and nicely distinguished by the use of brickwork.

At **Larbert** the railway is in cutting. The standard modern entrance, 1976, is, for once, not on an overbridge. Inside the stairs to the platform are housed in a glass box-like stair well this time entirely redeemed by an elegant verticality. The retention of the vintage footbridge provides balance and variety.

Maze Hill
1980

Stevenage
1977

Larbert
1979

Larbert 1979

The ultimate in 'slab roof' designs, **Birmingham International**, 1976, has most of its facilities at the higher, footbridge, level reached by stairs or escalators. From all points of view it is probably the most successful post-war station in the country. Direct access is provided to the National Exhibition Centre.

Glass boxes do not get better as they get bigger, but inside, **Bedford**, 1978, reveals the secret of the slab roof even though, externally, it does not have one.

In 1978 the West Midlands Transport Authority, in conjunction with British Rail, renewed the stations from Birmingham New Street to **Longbridge** with a series having a close family resemblance. **University** is typical. The most deviant is Northfield.

Birmingham International 1978

Birmingham International 1983

**Birmingham International
1983**

Right and below
Bedford Midland 1981

University 1985

In the following year the Glasgow transport authority, Trans-Clyde, completed the remodelling of its own Underground and, with British Rail, many other suburban stations. **Dalmarnock** shows the judicious elision of the British Rail and Trans-Clyde house styles. **Finnieston** has one of the most forbidding, not to say repellant, entrances imaginable. Inside, the modern decor is much more kindly. **Argyle Street** received the best modern station façade in Glasgow, and perhaps, in the country. It is a symmetrical composition of squares and rectangles suggesting, in the 1930s tradition, a classical order. Note also the dimensioning of the elements; classical Pythagorean proportions do not go out of date.

Dalmarnock 1981

Finnieston 1981

Argyle Street 1981

The stations of the Glasgow Underground, colloquially 'the Subway', were a family distinguished by the station name in orange lettering and each carried a large U. The basic design, as used at **Bridge Street**, West Street and Kinning Park, was otherwise not unlike the British Rail type used at Larbert. It could be expanded and given more than one entrance, as at **Ibrox**, or contracted to fit into an alley as at Kelvinhall. At Buchanan Street it was even pushed into a hole in the ground. The free-standing **Shields Road** was the prettiest and **Govan** certainly the largest.

The Tyne & Wear Metro is the product of another regional transport authority centred on Newcastle-upon-Tyne. Its stations are provided with a cubic logo carrying an M on each vertical face. Newly built stations are in two sizes. **Jesmond**, 1981, typifies the larger, housing a spacious automated booking hall in a glass box. In the city centre they may be subterranean. The smaller ones, like **Wallsend**, 1982, paradoxically have duplicate booking facilities either side of the line to avoid the need for interior footbridges or subways. Other stations lurk within converted ex-main line buildings.

Bridge Street 1981

Ibrox 1981

Shields Road 1981

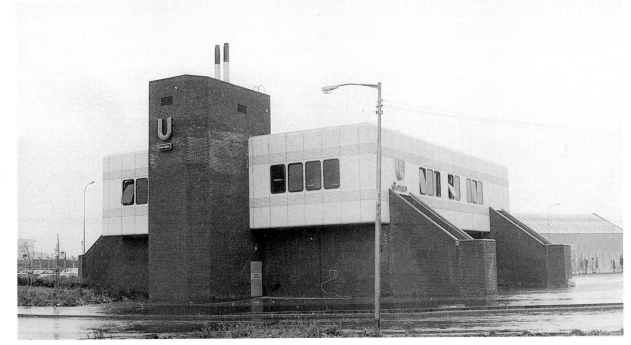

**Govan
1981**

*Left and
below*
**Jesmond
1984**

Wallsend 1984

Peterborough, 1980, was one of the last stations in the slab roof modern style with system glazing. Away from the entrance the frontage suffers from too much un-relieved walling. Even in-situ brickwork can be carried to excess. The interior, however, shows a very effective modern platform-scape.

Right and below
Peterborough 1983

Hendon had to be altered to accommodate the M1 motorway. In 1981 it was provided with a nice little one-off entrance slightly akin to the West Midlands style.

From a distance **Milton Keynes Central**, 1982, looks like a glass box to end all glass boxes. But objections, if any, should doubtless be addressed to the New Town rather than the railway. The station proper lies centrally, beneath a projecting slab motif. Inside, the booking hall and contemporary platform buildings are excellent. Suburban trains terminate here but bay platforms and buffers are eschewed in favour of the greater flexibility of extra through platforms.

Hendon 1982

Left and below
Milton Keynes 1985

Milton Keynes 1985

Knockholt had a standard SER timber building which was lost to fire. In 1985, a few years later, it was replaced by a type of building now being used widely over the system. It is substantially built of brick and has a glazed passenger entrance combining booking office and a limited covered waiting area. Where desired, this can equally well be placed intermediately in the building. There is a pitched, tiled roof overall giving an air of modest permanence.

True to the tradition that stations reflect the general fashions of secular architecture, post-modernism had come to the railway. Slab roofs are giving way to pitched expanses of tiles or slates. **Telford Central** (p. 2) can be regarded as transitional. The new **Derby**, completed in 1988, seems a good example to end on and, with Birmingham Curzon Street, makes good the promised span of 150 years of railway stations.

Knockholt 1986

Derby 1988

Index

N.B. Page numbers in italic refer to illustrations